TEA FRIED BRAIN

NOTES FROM SAINT CAMELLIA'S

CHURCH OF THE FIRST INFUSION

FRANK HADLEY MURPHY

ISBN:-13: 978-1493605644

ISBN-10: 149360564X

Printed by CreateSpace

For my children,

Kyrie Maria Murphy

and

Bennett Maverick Riversong Murphy

ACKNOWLEDGMENTS

I would like to thank the family of Michael Kevin O'Donnell for entrusting me with Michael's journals and for giving me permission to take liberties with those journals.

Madison Cawein, for designing the front cover of this book and for introducing me to the calligraphy of Wang Xizhi, (Wang Hsi-Chih, 303-361 AD) which appears on the front and back covers.

For art direction and layout for the front and back covers, my thanks to Faye and Patrick Bates.

Bea Yang, at Oolong Tea Square in Taiwan, for helping me find the only poem Li Po wrote about tea.

Steven Owyoung, for his comments on Wang Xizhi's calligraphy and for translating Li Po's (Li Bo) poem "Immortal's Palm Tea" from the original Chinese literary script.

Corax at his chadao.blogspot.com for permission to reprint Steven Owyoung's translation of Li Po's poem.

Wilderness guide, ceremonialist and wife, Carol Parker, for her knowledge of Vedic tradition and Andean cosmology.

Frederick Dannaway for his many extraordinary articles, essays and phone conversations about tea.

Traveling companion, David Baltzer, retired president of the hospital in Gallup, NM, where my son was born. It was David who offered up his chambers in Lijiang for experimenting with Yunnan's golden plant spirit tobacco medicine.

Jon Oscher, again, for his generosity.

I'd also like to thank Bob Wilson and Cynthia Lane.

And, for their editorial contributions, Faye Bates and Eda Gordon.

My apologies for the unrefined quality of this self-published text.

CONTENTS

THE CHAMA TAO

It was dark when I left Santa Fe. Orion was still chasing the Pleiades across the western heavens, first light was an hour away and the earth exuded the primal fragrance of the desert waking from its encounter with the night: moist adobe mixed with the dry decay of ponderosa pine.

Pulling north on US Highway 84 at 5 AM, I started climbing up the first grade outside of town into the sparse juniper and pinon pine woodlands. It was my intention to get to the river early enough to see some wildlife that may still be lingering along the water's edge.

I would stay on 84 through the towns of Espanola and Abiquiu, then, two and a half miles past Ghost Ranch, there was a forest service road that came in from the west.

US 84 doesn't continue much farther up the line from here. It passes through Chama, New Mexico, crosses the Continental Divide and the Colorado border and terminates in Pagosa Springs.

A respectable, transcontinental highway of 1,919 miles, it begins in Georgia, near the Atlantic Seaboard, and passes east to west through seven states.

84 enters New Mexico from Texas over the flat yet elevated plains of the Llano Escatado at the town of Texico, eight to ten miles east of Clovis. I've never felt obligated to visit Texico or its cross border counterpart of Farwell, Texas to satisfy my curiosity. I'll leave that to some other intrepid soul.

Through New Mexico 84 doesn't travel alone. It is joined for a while by US Highway 285 as it passes through Santa Fe and Espanola but if you were to stop your car, get out and take a look straight down at the pavement, you would not be able to tell which was which.

It is the section of 84 that runs between Santa Fe and Ghost Ranch, however, with which I am most familiar. I imagine it's one of the most spectacular stretches of highway in the U.S., passing, as it does, through the high desert canyon lands made famous by American artist, Georgia O'Keeffe.

The sun was still below the eastern horizon when I reached the forest service road. I pulled off 84, stopped, released my seat belt, turned off the headlights, rolled down the windows and proceeded down this old dirt road at ten miles an hour.

It was October and here the road was lined with purple asters, stands of reddish-orange Indian paintbrush and the varying yellow hues of wild sunflowers, snake weed and rabbit brush or chamiso.

Thirty years ago, you would see an occasional Datura growing in the ditches along this road but not any longer. They're such a mysterious-looking plant, standing sometimes five feet high with large, fragrant, trumpet-like flowers, that they were probably dug up by various pilgrims and hauled off to Minnesota or some such place. Most people know this member of the Nightshade family as Jimson Weed. The English know it as Thorn Apple. Homeopaths call it Stramonium and the local ranchers, locoweed. Carlos Castaneda wrote of it as a narcotic and hallucinogenic if prepared properly. If not, it could kill you.

Even though the Chihuahuan Desert is a lot closer, this whole area of northern New Mexico is classified as an Upper Sonoran Life Zone. It's a heading that always seemed a bit of a stretch to me as I'm sure it has to others who are familiar with the Sonoran Desert of Mexico and southern Arizona. The vegetation's completely different there because it's a lot lower. Cactus predominates but as you travel north of Phoenix the land rises, the vegetation changes to mixed conifers and it looks a lot like New Mexico. In other words, I won't suggest it be called anything else...at the moment.

While it may appear that scientists have been challenged to define exactly what kind of desert we are here in northern New Mexico, they have also been challenged by the weather, namely, how to predict it, and have even designated a new "forecasting area" for Santa Fe called "Santa Fe Metro." Well, we don't feel too "metro" here. A friend of mine jokes that when you consider that most of the state's meteorologists have been institutionalized or incarcerated over the years because of their inability to forecast the weather in the Santa Fe area, you begin to have some compassion for them. He exaggerates, but life here can seem exaggerated at times. It can appear to be concentrated, magnified. Part of this is due to the fact that we are at the confluence of two opposing geological and climatological zones: mountains and desert. The weather's changeable, hard to predict and like the landscape very dramatic. There are times when you can get a tan in a snowstorm or have to wear sunglasses in the rain. Mark Twain once wrote of New England weather that if you didn't like it, wait ten minutes and it would change, but as a native New Englander I never found this to be true. Instead, I found it applied more accurately to the weather systems of the American Southwest. What I'm trying to say is that there's some very unusual phenomenon happening in northern New Mexico that is more than the sum of colliding external forces.

Forest Service Road 151 is 13 miles long. Initially, to the north, or off to your right as you enter, you drive along the magnificent white, yellow and red sandstone walls of the Mesa de las Viejas, Mesa of the Old Women. These walls are the northwest boundary of the Piedra Lumbre Basin, the Piedra Lumbre Spanish Land Grant, or The Valley of Shining Stone. To the south, or to your left, are open and rolling tracts of grama grass and sagebrush.

The dominant geological feature here is the 9,862 foot, truncated peak of Cerro Pedernal (Flint Hill, or Flint Mountain). From a distance, Pedernal looks like it might have a flat, circular top, but when you climb up there -- and there's only one way up -- you see that there are different elevations: rocky, open spaces, wooded glades and a very narrow path along a ridge line that drops right off on either side.

I first went there with an archeologist who was looking for the old flint quarry that Native Americans mined for
their arrow and ax heads. He knew exactly where it was,
thanks to his lensatic compass and topo map. The quarry
was still being used, as far as we could tell, by the local
peoples. And the flint, which lay everywhere in various
chipping stations, is gorgeous. Pieces may be found that are
pure, unblemished white, deep dark red and opaque to
translucent black.

About four miles in, the road swings to the northwest
and drops down onto the canyon floor. The road has been
upgraded constantly since I first drove it in 1978. At that
time, a rain would render it impassable even for a four-
wheel-drive vehicle. Anyone in these parts who knows the
road has their own stories of being stuck in the mud for
hours, or days at a time.

Seven miles in, Skull Bridge crosses the river. Since
31 miles of this riparian habitat was declared a Wilderness
Area by the federal government in 1978 and six miles of that
a Wild and Scenic River in 1986, the bridge remains locked
and the land protected.

Another five miles and the road ends at the Monastery
of Christ in the Desert, a Benedictine abbey of about 25
monks that has been there since the mid-sixties. The
towering glass panels of the chapel, designed by Japanese
American woodworker and architect, George Nakashima, are
dwarfed by the 900 foot sandstone cliffs immediately behind
it. It is an image one never forgets. Beyond the monastery,
the canyon narrows into a gorge. Access is non-existent, but
in the summer months rafters float down the river past the
monastery from El Vado Dam.

The canyon below the monastery is open year round
to hikers and campers. On summer evenings, the sweet,
fragrant smoke of pinon and juniper campfires rises through
the cottonwoods and wafts downriver. Directly across from
the monastery, the Gallina River comes in through its own
canyon, whose access is also closed to the public. Now, in
the fall, this bottomland was filled with the golden foliage of

gigantic cottonwood trees set off by the multicolored sandstone walls of this, the Chama River Canyon.

It was Wednesday morning and I pulled into the Oak
Grove at 7 AM. I got out of my car and walked out to the
cliff edge above the river. The water was so thick with mud
and clay that it moved through the canyon like slurry. It was
potter's slip, so soft and silky that I just wanted to slide into
this moving mud bath and float away with it.

The sun was just lifting off the eastern rim of the
canyon and when the warmth of that desert sun hit me my
whole body rejoiced. Even the birds seemed to have come
alive in the warmth and brilliance of the morning light. As
the sun rose, the colors and the smells of the canyon became
more intense. Permeating everything was the damp earth
aroma of wet willow thickets. For what seemed like a half an
hour, I found myself dazzled, transfixed by the fragrances
and beauty surrounding me.

After a few moments, I walked back to my van and
parked it face out toward the road to let people know that
this space had been claimed for the day. I then opened the
hatch of my van and removed two chairs and a pair of binoculars. They were not folding deck chairs but pieces of
heavy patio furniture with cushions for some "serious sitting." If I were going to be here for a while, I liked to be
comfortable. I carried them out to a bluff 14 feet above the
river with open views of the canyon, which, at this point, was
so narrow that it also afforded me an awareness of people
coming and going on the road.

I came to the canyon about once a month and was
prepared to stay overnight, or several days if I got stuck in
the mud. Rain and snow were always a problem. In the
winter months, if there was snow, it was advisable to arrive
early in the morning while the road was still frozen and then
exit after the frosts had set in.

The Oak Grove wasn't far off the road but what made
the place unique were the oaks themselves. They were bent
over so far their tops touched the ground. They formed a
shaded archway where, for years, I'd pitch a tent. There were
many oaks on the river. Some grew in circles arching over

backwards away from the center like a fountain. These Gambel Oaks grew in colonies that spread from their root system more than from acorns. The arching effect, I believe, was a result of phototropism.

I loved these trees. Oaks played an integral part in the creation myths of my northern European ancestry and I identified with them more than I ever could with the Judeo-Christian archetypes of the Middle East.

So I plunked the chairs down, shifted them about to stabilize them on the uneven ground and sat.

The Chama River Canyon Wilderness is almost completely contained within the Santa Fe National Forest. Immediately behind my chair, however, there is a corner of the Carson National Forest that drops down into the canyon claiming a square mile or two. This drop is dramatic. My chair sits at 6,400 feet but the canyon walls all around me rise to over 8,000.

The Chama River is only 130 miles long. Its headwaters rise just over the Colorado border much like where US Highway 84 terminates. It flows into the Rio Grande five miles north of Espanola, near where New Mexico's original capital, San Juan de los Caballeros, was situated in 1598.

A breeze picked up and I found myself staring at the wind in the trees on the far side of the river but my attention was distracted by movement at my feet. A tarantula spider had just walked out from beneath my chair. These spiders "migrate" in the autumn; it's often the only time you see these mostly nocturnal creatures. Because of their large size, they're hard to miss. Once on a fall evening, when I was driving along the southern rim of Canyon de Chelly in Arizona with my high beams on, I noticed hundreds of these creatures casting long shadows across the road. I didn't know what they were at first until I stopped the car and got out to take a look. They were male tarantulas looking for a mate so the term migration is not accurate here unless you're willing to consider bar hopping a form of migration. The specimen that had just walked out from beneath me passed through the grama grass and disappeared over the edge of the bluff, 90 degrees straight down.

The river was low today exposing vast open areas of sand bars and mud flats. Rafting season had ended and there were now fewer releases of water from El Vado Dam which was about 24 miles upriver as the raven flies or about 120 miles as the bat flies. In the warmer months, the Bureau of Reclamation releases a certain amount of water from El Vado Lake. I planned my trips to the canyon around those releases because it was a lot quieter in the canyon without the extra traffic on the road and on the river.   Since all of the releases were on the weekend, I simply came during the week. If not, and I happened to be there when the rafters and kayakers floated past in their colorful flotillas, I simply moved my chair back under the canopy of the oaks where I wasn't noticed.

It was shortly after I sat down at the cliff's edge that a beaver paddled past, holding close to the shore with a willow switch in its mouth. There were none of their traditional dams and lodges here. The river was too forceful and the amount of water in the river fluctuated dramatically from week to week. They, like the muskrats, had burrows in the riverbanks.

There was always something going on in the canyon. If I sat long enough in one spot it would often happen right before me. I never wanted to read or wander too far away from the river lest I miss something. Once when I began to doze off, I thought to myself that I had better not, something could happen. And then I heard the rushing sound of bird wings and a pair of bald eagles soared 20 feet directly over my head.

Several Canada Geese families had nests across from me. They were here now for the winter. Last year there were three pairs of bald eagles in the canyon and in the dead of winter I'd watch them stalk the geese up and down the river.

The river attracted a host of migrating waterfowl -- sand pipers, mallards, etc. The male and female mergansers were the most strikingly handsome couple I've ever seen in the bird kingdom – gracious, fashionable, erudite. My fa-vorite, however, was the Great Blue Heron when it drifted in from the left and sailed absolutely motionless for 1,000 yards across the entire landscape before disappearing behind an island in the river.

Once while nodding off in my chair, I heard the crunch and snap of footsteps over dried oak leaves behind me. I turned to witness 12 wild turkeys passing through my campsite. I got up slowly and followed behind them for a while. They didn't seem to mind.

The wild and crazy trickster birds, however, are the ravens. Soaring effortlessly in the warm thermal air currents they are the most playful of birds. One author calls them flying monkeys. I love to watch their angling antics with their 360 degree barrel rolls. One day, I saw one flying upside down with his feet straight up in the air and right on top of him, his mate. They had locked their feet, their bellies inches apart and flew for some distance parallel to the ground.

For all the fancy birds in the canyon there will always be a special place in my heart for robins and sparrows. They were birds I grew up with in New England. When I first got to New Mexico it delighted me no end to see that some robins wintered over here. To this day, I still rejoice when I see them kicking around in the snow like a towhee in the leaves beneath a bush. We didn't see that in New England because they went south for the winter. Their return was one of the first signs of spring. Here in the canyon, robins are always the very last birdcall I hear at night. It's a comforting call, a perky, reassuring chirp.

By late morning I grew hungry, got up out of my chair, walked over to the van and pulled out a number of canvas bags. I carried them all over to the oaks and put them down on the ground in the shade. The trees acted as a windbreak. I grabbed a container of food out of one of the bags and went to river's edge to eat. After a while, when my blood sugar stabilized and the taste of food had left my mouth, I began to think about making tea.

Often times, the thought, the desire to have tea, the decision to move in that direction shifted my consciousness and signaled that the ritual had already begun. Part of that shift was to move my attention from the natural world that surrounded me, the expanded awareness of nature observation, to the focused discipline of an inner landscape that was required for any practice. So I got up out of my chair again, walked into the trees where I'd placed my tea bag and plunked myself right down on the ground.

I first made a clearing in the dirt by brushing away the season's debris: twigs, acorns, dead leaves and grasses. I then set the stove up by wiggling the base of it into the dirt to make it level. It was a single burner backpacking stove with a small butane tank. I spread out the metal pot supports and placed an empty saucepan upon them. Over the years, living in this desert clime, I grew to appreciate water more and more because of its scarcity. My understanding of it, my relationship with it, approached reverence. So when I heard Thich Nat Hahn's simple prayer for water, I adopted it as my own and spoke it now as I poured water into my pan: *"Water flows from high in the mountains, water runs deep in the earth. Miraculously water comes to us and sustains all life. Thank you, water."*

I next unfolded the flame adjuster, turned it on till I heard gas escaping, struck a match and lit her up. Under my breath I said these words: *"I call upon the spirits of the wind to stir the flames of my fire. I call upon the spirits of the fire to heat my water and I call upon the spirits of the water to help make my tea."*

These words were inspired by the three trigrams on a brazier that was owned by China's patron saint of tea, Lu Yu. One trigram was for wind, another for fire and the last for water.

Next, I unwrapped a bamboo tray and placed it on the ground as well. Upon the tray I put a porcelain gaiwan, a few wooden implements and a cup, a Chinese teacup, without handle or saucer.

It never takes long for water to boil with certain backpacking stoves. So when it started boiling, I lifted the pan off the flame with one of those contoured potholders that slip right over the handle and poured warming water into the gaiwan and the cup. I put the pan back on the stove and poured the water from these vessels onto the ground at the foot of the trees. I then lifted a disk of pressed tea from its box, removed the protective paper just enough to expose one end and inserted a knife made from the rib of an ox, that was designed for this maneuver, into the side of this Puerh, or Puer, cake and twisted it. I broke off some tea, dropped it into the warmed gaiwan and poured the boiling water over the leaves. I then took the lid of the gaiwan, dipped it into the hot water at the bottom of the saucepan to warm it up and placed it over the brewing leaves. As the steam pressure built beneath the lid, it pressed down on the water raising the level of the brew and made it overflow into the saucer. At the same time, air trapped in this old cake began to be released and the lid of the gaiwan would sometimes pop and clatter about.

Parting with tradition, I rarely rinsed the leaves before brewing them because I considered rinsing to be a "deficit disorder." The thinking was this: if I were to rinse these leaves, if I were to pour water over them briefly and throw that water out, I would also be throwing out some of the tea's nutrients, some of the taste, some of the caffeine, theo-bromine, theophyline and L-Theanine, but most importantly, I would also be throwing out a portion of the tea's vital life force, it's chi. However brief the rinse, the leaves will be in a depleted state before we even take our first sip and our experience will be compromised. The other thing is that no one could adequately explain to me the whole tradition of rinsing, when it started, why people did it. So why begin your relationship with a new tea at a deficit? It's disruptive to the leaves and to the process. Friends, however, did not agree.

And now, while the leaves brewed, I placed my hand over the vessel and said a few more words: "*Bless this tea and bless this water, may this union be made in heaven. I call upon the spirit of the leaf, the devas of the plant and the soul of the species to waken from your slumber and impart upon these waters the wisdom of the earth and I shall endeavor to create within myself a receptive vessel within which to receive that wisdom.*" Then in silence, I held my hand over the leaves and ran my energy and intention, my love and gratitude, down through my palm and into the brew.

After four minutes, I decanted into the teacup, retaining the leaves with the lid of the gaiwan. I then poured a little of the tea onto the ground in an offertory gesture of thanks and went back to my perch above the river with this dense, black sludge.

I let the tea rest, let it cool for a few minutes in my lap, for even though the leaves have been pulled from the brew, there was still particulate matter in the tea to keep it infusing for a while longer. This, plus how the tea cools, is what can cause a tea to taste different with every sip.

With the first sip, there is a second shift in consciousness as my whole body fills with the essence of the leaf. I make tea in an empty vessel and then I become an empty vessel to receive it. The practice of maintaining this emptiness is a practice that runs through all of the world's mystical traditions. In the West, there is a prayer that goes: *Lord, make me decrease so that you might increase in me.* The point is to get out of our own way and become a kind of receiver for whatever is to come. We take that first sip and open to it, yield to it and let it affect us. Tea has now begun to infuse us. This ritual of making and tasting tea can then become what I call an entry ritual, a doorway into other realms. That is why I write of tea as an entheogen, a substance that is capable of creating the sensation of the divine within or that causes one to become inspired or to experience feelings of inspiration. With the first taste I encounter the silken viscosity, the floral notes and dried, fruity tones, the earthen depths, wooded bite and all of it bathing my tongue with waves of unfolding complexity before it slides down the back of my throat. "Waves of cascading epiphanies" may be more accurate, for such is the way it feels when tea stirs us to our soul, sharing with us her deepest mysteries.

I begin to notice a number of opening sensations in my tummy and then, as my body and the tea continue to shift and mobilize in union with each other, there are these opening, flowering sensations in my heart: open, expansive

11

feelings of love and joy. So in a way, it may be said that tea flowers twice, once on the bush and a second time in our hearts. And so she stirs. And she mobilizes.

I sat for a long while savoring the whole body sensations a well-aged Pu-erh imparts. I followed the warmth of the tea down into my belly where it has pooled and where it seems, not only to activate every pore on my skin, but flown out through those pores, looking, perhaps, for its way back home.

The tea pulls me back so far into myself that my senses became attuned to a different set of coordinates, a different set of phenomenon. Perhaps it is that my senses align themselves with a subtle, more refined resonance. One that is silent and still. Perhaps a part of this shift in consciousness is what is meant when it is said that tea muffles strident noises. I do not know. I am not a scientist. I have never been known for my powers of deductive reasoning. I would prefer to lie down under tea bushes on the green, terraced hills of Yunnan...and dream. Dream as I dreamt now in this altered state, feeling the tea leading me through doorways coupled with the mesmerizing sun sparkling on the water.

In this reverie I sat all day and watched the water flow past. From time to time, a trout would jump up out of the water. A deer emerged from a willow thicket for a moment to drink, looked about and disappeared back into that thicket. As evening approached out came the swifts and swallows, the owls and the bats, nighthawks...and rattlesnakes.

I sat and the hours passed as I dropped into the exquisite luxury of silence and solitude. Here, my mind quiets naturally, little will is involved.

Nature observation can be exhausting as you sit motionless for long periods with all your senses heightened, acutely aware of any unusual noises or movements, any changes in "the field" before you. It's really a state of hyper-vigilance with all of its associated fatigue. You sit still for so long that small birds fly over to land on your head. You flinch, they catch themselves, do a 180 mid-air, fly back to the branch where they were and shake off the fright.

So the shadows lengthen and the wind shifts, alternately coming up the canyon and blowing down, reminding me of the land and sea breezes on the island of Martha's Vineyard. During the day, a light breeze would blow in from the sea and at night, as the land cooled, breezes blew across the island out to sea. Here in the canyon, however, the prevailing winds were from the north and west and all the leaves from the oaks were pushed back in upon themselves, away from the river and into the trees and there they stayed all winter.

I sat and watched the last of the sun disappear below the western rim of the canyon. The temperature dropped ten degrees and I was in shade but the cliffs behind me were still ablaze and above them clouds sailed on in the brilliance of daylight. Another hour and the cliffs themselves softened in shadow and the whole canyon filled with a pink glow from a sunset that illuminated the entire sky. Now it was the heavens turn to have caught fire. The day had been a light show and in the warmth that radiated from all the rocks around me, I left my perch above the river and went for a walk along the road.

One of the first things I noticed when I came to Santa Fe was when walking through town after dark on cold November evenings. I'd be strolling along somewhere and I would walk into a pocket of warmth ten to twenty degrees above the air temperature. It was always the adobe wall beside me that had retained the heat of the day. So I'd pause there for a while and, if I were not rushed, I'd press my body into its heat. It was like that now as I walked down the road. The temperatures continued to drop but large boulders offered an incandescence all their own.

The road was hard, compacted dirt and it was easy to work up a stride. At this hour deer came down from the mesas for a drink but there were none now, no coyotes or foxes, just silence and stillness as the canyon shifted into its own mysteries, its own solitude.

I headed back to my roost and sat down. It was dinnertime and I'd have a few more spoonfuls of what was left from lunch. Then I waited till the first owls started to

13

dialogue back and forth across the canyon from each other. One leapt out of a dead cottonwood near me, grabbed a bat in flight and flew back to the tree to eat it. The beavers came out at this time, too, paddling up river to gather more willow switches.

As darkness descended, the last silhouettes over the water were angling bats feeding on mosquitoes.

I got up out of my chair, went up to the van and got my bedding items which I carried back to the shelter of the oaks. I also grabbed a few flashlights of varying intensity. With one of these flashlights, I scanned the ground for rocks and branches and kicked a few things off to one side.

I took off most of my clothes and got in my bag. There was no need for a hat at this time of year. It was still warm. In the winter, when it got below zero and I was sleeping here on the ground, under the stars, I'd wear either a rabbit fur hat that snapped under my chin or a down face mask that pulled over my head with two slits for my eyes and one for my nose.

Settled in my bag, lying on my back, I folded a pillow up under my head and watched the sky for a while. There were shooting stars, satellites, the silent passage of an airliner with a vapor trail drifting off behind it and an occasional low cloud passing before the stars as it looked for a place to harbor in the canyon for the evening.

I then listened to all the sounds of the canyon: owls, coyotes, nighthawks, a vole darting under the leaves next to my bed. I also knew that a rattler or two might pass by in the middle of the night on their way down to the river. They have before, but they, like black widow spiders, keep to themselves. My only concerns were mosquitoes, but even they were not out in numbers tonight. Perhaps they, too, were sitting in the branches of nearby trees looking out at the wonder of the desert sky.

I always slept better here, on the ground, cradled by the earth. I felt protected by the oaks and the canyon's massive walls. It was a balm to my soul this sleeping under the stars. There was a healing quality about this land. Some of it was the energy of the place, some the negative ions of turbulent water, some the slow, soothing pace of the river but I always felt different when I woke, as if a great calm had descended upon me.

The weariness of the long day began to affect me. I closed my eyes and took a number of long, deliberate breaths. How I fell asleep determined how I slept and how I woke and I wanted to wake bright and clear. Simple breathing exercises were often insurance that I would wake with the foundation I needed for the next day.

II

"IF GOD IS YOUR FRIEND, FIRE IS YOUR WATER."
RUMI

It was a different river I woke to in the morning. It had come alive and rushed past with such urgency that I threw back my bed covers, got up and walked out to the cliff. There had been a release in the middle of the night and the water was a foot over what had greeted me the day before. There were no sand bars or mud flats now.

The color of the water had changed as well. It was dark red, suggesting that somewhere up river a number of clay cliffs had collapsed into the water.

With more water in the canyon, the river was loud, rich, vibrant, as it scrambled over boulders and splashed about. The moisture in the air was palpable, saturated with the fragrance of oak leaves, sage and wet willow. In these hours, I'd take great draughts of the morning air for nothing else invigorated me in the same way.

After a few moments I went back to my bedroll and lay down. With the desert's thin air and intense sunlight, I was already in an altered, rarified state long before I had any tea.

My senses were always heightened in nature. It was a state of vigilance comparable to falling asleep with one ear cocked toward my children's rooms; a mental, a physical acuity where my whole body was a radar screen. I laid there and stared at the canyon walls. The cliffs vibrated in the desert sun and I was riveted by their beauty.

After a while, I got up from my bed, walked again out to my chair at the cliff and sat in silence for the rest of the morning.

At noon a car drove past stirring me from my reverie. It was moving methodically up the road as if looking for a place to pull in. I wondered if it were a gaggle of artists in search of a place to settle for the day. It is difficult enough to try to describe this landscape but how do you begin to paint it? For yes, there is a vast array of colors in the dramatic topography of Abiquiu and the Chama River Canyon that draw artists from all over the world but the desert is unlike other places to paint. Friends have said that they may finish a study of a few muted, dusty green hills in the morning and, as the sun rises and the light intensifies, the colors change and so does their frustration. The sun crosses the afternoon, and the yellow ochre striations and white limestone caps of the Dakota Formation step out of their shadowy recess and begin to align themselves with our nervous systems. Pathologies become accentuated and eventually we realize the impact this supernatural beauty is having upon us. Our bodies become tense from the dryness, lack of oxygen and startling ferocity of the light. It strips us down. On hot summer afternoons it's a conspiracy. Everything gathers to consume us.

It is the red iron oxide cliffs and clay hills that are the most unstable as they move from pink corals and salmons in the morning to cinnabar or vermillion in the afternoon. The reds get magnified and begin to pulsate with their own power of the place. The cliffs around you seem to catch fire, melt and bleed into the river.

Absentmindedly, the artist may lay her brush down and wander out into the sage for a few hours wondering what has made everything so bright, all lit up. And why does her heart feel so tense with growth, as if it were about to explode? And then, about four, clouds move in from the west to offer a moment of respite from this explicit terrain. A cool breeze passes through our clothes and we remember why we came.

In his book "The Solace of Fierce Landscapes," that recount some of his own experiences in the Chama River Canyon and at Ghost Ranch, Belden Lane writes about how "....the austere, heart breaking beauty of this desert scape strips you down, disarms you and silences you with it's incredible indifference." "It's a place," he writes, "where people confront their own edges because in wild places, terror and growth-toward-wholeness walk hand in hand."

"It is a place that is intrinsically hostile to the ego because you quickly come to the end of what you have depended upon to give continuity and meaning to your life. A scape whose emptiness is as exhilarating as it is frightening." "The long, silent contemplation of a vast, indifferent terrain has been shown, throughout human experience, to be a powerful force in subverting self-consciousness, pushing the outer edges of language, evoking the deepest desire of the human heart for untamed mystery and beauty." "It is a deep mystery" he continues, "that love is born in the mind's (and body's) experience of emptiness and loss." And again "Prayer without words can only begin where loss is reckoned as total." Where "...abandonment is perceived not only as a loss but also as a grace."

These were eloquent and profound words. Reading them again, trying them on, their very tone wears me down and that's the point. I permit myself to be stripped down because I know that it will bring me to a place of such emptiness and vulnerability the only thing that remains is love.

In 2008, I was so exhausted, so depleted by the emotional stress in my life that it was easy to sit by the river for hour upon hour, day upon day and not have a single thought come into my mind. All day, the wind, the water and the clouds drifted down the canyon, and my thoughts, if there were any, drifted down the river with them.

When I needed to get out of town and be alone, this is where I came. It was my respite space, a place I'd been coming to for 35 years. Once, during a particularly difficult time, I pulled into the grove, opened the door of my car and fell out onto the ground with my feet still up in the cab. I laid there for a long time, feeling all my energy, my strength, drain out into the earth. After a while, the movement re-versed itself and the energy returned in an altered, augment-ed form. This new energy from the earth revived me so that, after another short while, I realized I had enough strength to get up.

It was not so much this sensation of bleeding or draining into the earth that intrigued me but the emptiness

18

which resulted because I knew that it is only by virtue of our emptiness that we can receive.

In Tan Dun's opera "Tea: A Mirror of Soul" there are several scenes where a monk drinks from an empty tea bowl as if to fill himself with its emptiness.

It is a natural consequence for things to enter into the spaces that have been provided for them. If we invoke, if we supplicate, if we invite things into these spaces, then we should not be surprised by what comes forth. They may not be things from the external world necessarily but from our very own wisdom base where that still, small voice resides.

This practice of emptying and then residing in that emptiness, where I would sit in a sort of pure absence without any expectation, as Rumi describes it, is a place where "words become an encumbrance to my thoughts."

This canyon was the container that held me over the last 35 years. It, too, was a vessel cut 1,800 feet into the earth where my heart and soul were refined, purified, reduced, as in a crucible, for crucibles are also vessels, often made of porcelain, used for melting substances at high temperatures. The crucibles I remember from high school chemistry all looked like little white Chinese tea cups except they had their own covers that fit over the rim of the crucible itself, unlike a gaiwan where the lid fit down inside the vessel.

You never hear or see the word crucible applied to tea, the tea process or its effects upon us because it's a different process. Or is it?

As I write about the alembics of internal tea experiences, I'm reminded of how we all are, really, in a crucible undergoing extraordinary refining and conversion processes, whether we have anything in our body's assisting us in this process or not. This experience of emptying, of emptiness, dropping down to the bottom of my soul became my own practice and sometimes an arduous one at that for there can be a challenging journey associated with such endeavors.

For example, I cannot attempt to create an empty, receptive space at the core of my being without dealing with, say, unresolved emotional issues. This process may involve

19

dropping through layers of loneliness, grief and heartache before I can gain access to what may feel like absolute zero, before I fall onto this bedrock of my being. Sometimes it takes minutes, sometimes hours, sometimes days. But as I journey forth, I create new pathways in my soul, a way my heart remembers, and the way becomes less difficult.

Over the years, as this practice deepened, as I gave myself over to it, love began to flow into these spaces with such power and force that I was seized by states of ecstasy. My whole body would fill with love which then poured out of me into the world, into the trees, the wildlife and the sky. I had the sensation of being lifted up off the ground and dragged forward. There was no other way to describe it than a seizure because I was possessed by this all-consuming power of love. I felt like I was experiencing the binding force of all nature, the fabric of the universe, total fulfillment and completion as a human being..........exaltation!

What felt like soft flames swept through my body consuming everything, burning indiscriminately. I had a say in nothing. The insides of my heart and mind were burned out, synapses were destroyed and recreated. Judgments, grief, loneliness, heartache, emotional history, even physical pain were all fired up in this furnace, this crucible my body had become.

These were incredibly cleansing, cathartic sensations to be consumed in such a way.

Each episode, each seizure, cleared out more and more and I began to feel reduced to the base plate of my being which, I felt, was the seat of my own personal power and wisdom..........the seat of my own divinity.

These ecstatic states even came in my sleep. Reading and writing about them also brought them on.

My efforts became focused on how to replicate these experiences, re-enter them at will.

In these spaces, it felt like my brain chemistry had been altered. My whole body changed and I felt like a different person. I was seized by the wonder, the power and the glory of the love that welled up inside me and then the profound sense of compassion that emanated from me out into the world.

Dictionaries describe ecstasy with such phrases as: "exalted delight where normal understanding is felt to be surpassed," "a state of any emotion so intense that rational thought and self-control are obliterated," "extreme personal well-being," "attainment of an elevated state permitting superhuman sensory or emotional experience." It is all of these things and more.

I felt no spirit near, no angels, no superior intelligence, because the source of this love was from every fiber of my own body. And neither was it centered in my heart as many would think. It engaged all of my corporeal being. It suggested to me that, without exception, all of humanity, everything on the earth, animate and inanimate, was composed of love, a love that preceded us as a species.

And neither was this something that I "channeled." It did not come down through my "crown chakra" from heaven above but radiated out from my entire body. It's source was myself and I was seized by ecstatic states more and more as I opened to them and let them affect me, transform me, the very same way I let tea revolutionize my heart and soul.

Sometimes I felt so much love I knew that if my days were at an end I could die satisfied, fulfilled as a human being, because this was the ultimate human experience.

The aspect of the experience of ecstasy that's never addressed, however, is what I call "the devastation of ecstasy," incredible loss as a result of this massive conflagration. Especially if the fires continue, they burn what they burn, they consume what they consume. It's not like we've raked up these nice little piles of leaves to set on fire. It's not like curbside pick-up. These were wildfires supplemented by "storms" of raging crown fires. That said, at one point, I felt like I was sitting in front of a roaring campfire, throwing things into it I didn't want. Another point, after the fires had burned themselves out, I wanted to go back and poke around in the ashes to see if there was anything salvageable but there were no ashes. Nothing. Just silence, stillness, cleanliness, just myself, alone, in the wilderness.

21

Years later, the effects of these fires were still affecting me. They were the long range effects of ecstasy that continued to alter how I thought, how I felt about things.

Still, they were always close at hand. Sometimes when I opened my arms up wide I could just walk into them.

I heard a ker-plop. Something had fallen into the water. I looked up and saw nothing. Besides a beaver jumping into the river from a height of two feet, there was only one other noise that sounded like that, a segment of river bank had fallen into the water. It happened all the time, especially across from me where the river ate into the embankment.

I scan the river and a Western Tanager flew out of the willow rushes capturing my attention with its bright red and yellow coloring. I followed this little flitting light show till it disappeared into some nearby cottonwoods.

Gazing up river, the Mesa Golondrina towered above both the Chama and the Gallina Rivers. Cloud shadows drifted in silence across its sheer cliff face, its rock wall.

Cool breezes blew down river and evaporated the sweat on my forehead and under my clothes. The refreshing breezes wakened me and I sat up, straightening my back with a sense of anticipation.

Another line of Belden Lane's popped into my head: "In early monastic practice, the desert served a double function of comforting the afflicted as well as afflicting the comfortable." It was in this context that I began to think of Michael O'Donnell and why I had come to the river.

III

POEMS

Michael had been a friend and colleague. His family had contacted me to see if I would be interested in editing and publishing his journals. I said I was and received them a few weeks ago but waited till now to open them because it was exactly a year ago today that I last saw Michael alive, here, at the river.

It was a box of spiral notebooks, oak tag folders and loose papers. On top were a number of poems. It was a place to begin.

The first poem was by Palestinian poet, Taha Mohammed Ali, who had been in Santa Fe a few years before. It was called:

TEA AND SLEEP

IF, OVER THIS WORLD, THERE'S A RULER
WHO HOLDS IN HIS HAND BESTOWAL AND
SEIZURE,
AT WHOSE COMMAND SEEDS ARE SEWN,
AS WITH HIS WILL THE HARVEST RIPENS,
I TURN IN PRAYER, ASKING HIM
TO DECREE FOR THE HOUR OF MY DEMISE,
WHEN MY DAYS DRAW TO AN END,
THAT I'LL BE SITTING AND TAKING A SIP
OF WEAK TEA WITH A LITTLE SUGAR
FROM MY FAVORITE GLASS
IN THE GENTLEST SHADE OF THE LATE
AFTERNOON
DURING THE SUMMER.

AND IF NOT TEA AND AFTERNOON,
THEN LET IT BE THE HOUR
OF MY SWEET SLEEP JUST AFTER DAWN.
AND MAY MY COMPENSATION BE
IF IN FACT I SEE COMPENSATION-
I WHO DURING MY TIME IN THIS WORLD
DIDN'T SPLIT OPEN AN ANT'S BELLY,
AND NEVER DEPRIVED AN ORPHAN OF MONEY,
DIDN'T CHEAT ON MEASURES OF OIL
OR VIOLATE A SWALLOW'S VEIL;
WHO ALWAYS LIT A LAMP
AT THE SHRINE OF OUR LORD, SHIHAB-A-DIN,
ON FRIDAY EVENINGS, AND NEVER SOUGHT TO
BEAT MY FRIENDS
OR NEIGHBORS AT GAMES,
EVEN THOSE I SIMPLY KNEW:
I WHO STOLE NEITHER WHEAT NOR GRAIN
AND DID NOT PILFER TOOLS
WOULD ASK-
THAT NOW, FOR ME, IT BE ORDAINED
THAT ONCE A MONTH,
OR EVERY OTHER,
I BE ALLOWED TO SEE THE ONE
MY VISION HAS BEEN DENIED-
SINCE THAT DAY I PARTED
FROM HER WHEN WE WERE YOUNG.
BUT AS FOR THE PLEASURES OF THE WORLD TO
COME,
ALL I'LL ASK
OF THEM WILL BE-
THE BLISS OF SLEEP, AND TEA.

The second was in a woman's handwriting. It was a
Coleman Barks "version" of Rumi's

THE CIRCLE AROUND THE ZERO

A LOVER DOESN'T FIGURE THE ODDS.
HE FIGURES HE CAME CLEAN FROM GOD
AS A GIFT WITHOUT A REASON,
SO HE GIVES WITHOUT CAUSE
OR CALCULATION OR LIMIT.

A CONVENTIONALLY RELIGIOUS PERSON
BEHAVES A CERTAIN WAY
TO ACHIEVE SALVATION.

A LOVER GAMBLES EVERYTHING, THE SELF,
THE CIRCLE AROUND THE ZERO!
HE OR SHE CUTS AND THROWS IT ALL AWAY.
THIS IS BEYOND ANY RELIGION.
LOVERS DO NOT REQUIRE FROM GOD ANY PROOF,
OR ANY TEXT, NOR DO THEY KNOCK ON A DOOR TO
MAKE SURE THIS IS THE RIGHT STREET.

THEY RUN,

AND THEY RUN.

Another Rumi poem followed.

THINKING AND THE HEART'S MYSTICAL WAY

A PEACEFUL FACE TWISTS WITH THE POISONOUS
NAIL OF THINKING.

A GOLDEN SPADE SINKS INTO A PILE OF DUNG.

SUPPOSE YOU LOOSEN AN INTELLECTUAL KNOT?

THE SACK IS EMPTY.

YOU'VE GROWN OLD TRYING TO UNTIE SUCH
TIGHTENINGS,

SO LOOSEN A FEW MORE, WHY KNOT?

THERE IS A BIG ONE FASTENED AT YOUR THROAT,
THE PROBLEM OF WHETHER YOU'RE IN HARMONY
WITH THAT WHICH HAS NO DEFINITION. SOLVE
THAT!

YOU EXAMINE SUBSTANCE AND ACCIDENTS.

YOU WASTE YOUR LIFE MAKING SUBJECT AND VERB
AGREE.

YOU EDIT HEARSAY.

YOU STUDY ARTIFACTS AND THINK YOU KNOW THE
MAKER, SO PROUD OF HAVING FIGURED THE
DERIVATION.

LIKE A SCIENTIST YOU COLLECT DATA AND PUT FACTS
TOGETHER TO COME TO SOME CONCLUSION.

MYSTICS ARRIVE AT WHAT THEY KNOW
DIFFERENTLY: THEY LAY THEIR HEAD UPON A
PERSON'S CHEST AND DRIFT INTO THE ANSWER.

THINKING GIVES OFF SMOKE TO PROVE THE
EXISTENCE OF FIRE.

A MYSTIC SITS INSIDE THE BURNING.

THERE ARE WONDERFUL SHAPES IN RISING SMOKE
THAT IMAGINATION LOVES TO WATCH.

BUT IT'S A MISTAKE TO LEAVE THE FIRE FOR THAT
FILMY SIGHT.

STAY HERE AT THE FLAME'S CORE.

(I'm sorry, but that little edge of "specialness"
Coleman Barks projects into Rumi's poems doesn't exist in
ecstatic states. Barks appears, even on stage, to be
enchanted, dazzled by his own renditions.)

A fourth poem, by Wallace Stevens, still had a
comment attached to it that I had sent him a year or two ago.

TEA

WHEN THE ELEPHANT'S-EAR IN THE PARK
SHRIVELLED IN FROST,
AND THE LEAVES ON THE PATHS
RAN LIKE RATS,
YOUR LAMP-LIGHT FELL
ON SHINING PILLOWS,
OF SEA-SHADES AND SKY-SHADES
LIKE UMBRELLAS IN JAVA.

27

I like to think that this poem describes an oolong tea experience Stevens may have had. Here's a poem where Stevens captures "The OO of Long-ness." Think about it. Do you remember your first oolong experience, when the leaves unfurl and you see one whole tea leaf standing free from the others for the very first time? It's an "Ah-ha" experience. Oolong tea leaves can look like shriveled elephant ears when they're dry, when you first see the finished leaf. They run like rats when they sit at the bottom of your vessel and you pour boiling hot water over them. They scatter. If you brew and drink your tea in clear glass tumblers of some sort like a lot of Russian, Jewish and Arab people do then you're sure to see the varying colors or "shades" of the tea infusing. Depending on whether this "lamp-light" had a shade, it may have created a golden aura like the deep ambers of a tea. Once the leaves unfurl, they look like those giant banana leaves that people break off in, say Java, to use as umbrellas while they wait in the rain for a bus.

A second Wallace Stevens poem was more inscrutable. Michael had retained my comments about this poem as well.

TEA AT THE PALAZ DE HOON

NOT LESS BECAUSE IN PURPLE I DESCENDED
THE WESTERN DAY THROUGH WHAT YOU CALLED
THE LONELIEST AIR, NOT LESS WAS I MYSELF.
WHAT WAS THE OINTMENT SPRINKLED ON MY
BEARD?
WHAT WERE THE HYMNS THAT BUZZED BESIDE MY
EARS?
WHAT WAS THE SEA WHOSE TIDE SWEPT THROUGH
ME THERE?

OUT OF MY MIND THE GOLDEN OINTMENT RAINED,
AND MY EARS MADE THE BLOWING HYMNS THEY
HEARD.
I WAS MYSELF THE COMPASS OF THAT SEA:
I WAS THE WORLD IN WHICH I WALKED, AND WHAT I
SAW
OR HEARD OR FELT CAME NOT BUT FROM MYSELF;
AND THERE I FOUND MYSELF MORE TRULY AND
MORE STRANGE.

This reminded me of Proust's epiphany with tea and the madeleine. We've all had epiphanies where we have come to a deep reckoning with, and an appreciation of ourselves. Startling insights come in the stillness tea imparts and there's a certain self-acceptance, even forgiveness. Tea is a muse. She's a woman, after all. Perhaps his "golden ointment" is the golden salve or balm that tea is for many of us. Perhaps, as he was drinking, a few drops fell on his beard glistening gold in a morning light. Perhaps also, this is just the farfetched musings of a tea mind.

Several years ago an acquaintance of mine said that her four year old son really liked his black tea. I was shocked that she gave him any tea at all at his age so I inquired. She said it was half tea, half whipping cream and two tablespoons of honey. I understood. She also shared that when he put his first pair of sunglasses on, which were those cheap polarized amber things, he exclaimed that the whole world looked like tea. Such is the way it can be for tea enthusiasts who interpret the world through tea-colored glasses.

The next two poems I had written and sent to Michael after my first wife died. I was surprised he still had them.

THE WORDLESS TAO

WHEN AARONE DIED

29

I CHOSE NOT TO REFERENCE
MY EXPERIENCES OF THE DIVINE
THROUGH CHRISTIANITY
THOUGH CHRISTIAN FRIENDS HELPED
SPAWN THOSE EXPERIENCES
WITH THEIR PRAYER.

EVEN AS A CHILD IN SUNDAY SCHOOL I KNEW
THERE WAS SOMETHING ELSE GOING ON
SOMETHING MORE GRAND
THAN WHAT I HEARD IN CHURCH.

THROUGHOUT MY LIFE
IT DID NOT MATTER FROM WHENCE
THESE EXPERIENCES CAME.
I DID NOT QUESTION THEM.
I WAS NOT CURIOUS.

THERE WAS NO PLACE FOR SCIENCE HERE,
NO GRAPPLING,
NO STRUGGLE TO DEFINE BECAUSE
THERE WAS NOT A WORD.
NOT A WORD

JUST A LOW CLOUD ON A MOUNTAIN LAKE.

EVENING MIST ROLLING UP A BEACH.

WHEN I DID SEEK
THE COMFORT AND COMPANY OF WORDS
IT WAS TO CHINA I TURNED.
CHINA.

WHERE ONE MAY STILL BATHE
IN THE FACELESS WORDS
OF THE WORDLESS TAO.

And another, written at the same time.

PERHAPS IT WAS THAT YOU AGREED
TO GO BEFORE LAST WE TEA'D
FOR ON THE STOVE AND IN THIS POT
WERE ROOTS AND TWIGS OF THIS AND NAUGHT
ITS CONTENTS ONLY YOU HAD KNOWN
FOR IN YOUR DREAMS IT WAS SHOWN
THAT HERE WITHIN THIS SEETHING BREW
YOUR LAST CUP WOULD HELP YOU THROUGH.
SO ON THE STOVE AND TO THIS DAY.
I BREW MY LEAVES WITH WHAT I PRAY
THAT WHEN I PASS I TOO WILL SEE
MY SOUL MOVING THROUGH MY TEA.

I lifted my eyes off the page and looked out across the river. A dust devil, about fifty feet high, was approaching the opposite shore. It dropped down a sandy bank onto the water and an explosive report echoed through the canyon. It was the sound of water being jerked up into the whirlwind. The collision gutted the dust devil and instantly this fifty foot pillar of dust collapsed into the river. I gazed off into the empty space left behind. My attention was then drawn to a red wing blackbird chasing a sand piper low over the river. The black bird came up right over the piper, raised its head and pecked it into the water. The sand piper, stunned, dazed, sat there a moment then lifted off into the sky.

Next was a ditty Michael wrote and sang to me here. This will introduce readers to Michael's wild and zany nature better than I.

"WOMEN IN THE KITCHEN BITCHIN' 'BOUT THEIR BEAUX.
TEA MAKES 'EM PEE WHEN THE CHI BEGINS TO FLOW.
MOODS BEGIN TO LIGHTEN WHEN THE SPIRIT STARTS TO BRIGHTEN,

31

IT'S THE OOLONG THAT TOOK TOO LONG FROM
THE CUP TO COMMODE.

MEN IN THE DEN THEY'RE SITTING AT THE
TUBE
TILL SAMMY BRINGS IN A POT A CHINA BREW.
OFF GOES THE TELLY WHEN LAUGHTER FILLS
THE BELLY,
HEARTS BEGIN TO SOFTEN WHEN YOU FEEL
LIKE A FOOL.

NOW THEY'RE ALL AWAKENED AND IT'S TIME
FOR MAKIN' UP.
LET'S MOVE 'EM TO THE PORCH TO PASS THE
CHINA CUP.
NOW WE'RE ALL INFUSIN' WHEN BEFORE WE
WERE REFUSIN'.
I TELL YOU IT'S THAT GODDESS IN THAT
TEKUANYIN.

A chorus went something like this:

"SO WHEN YOUR HEART'S A BROKIN'
YOUR JUICES ALL ARE CHOKIN'
IT MEANS YOUR BODY'S GROPIN'
FOR THAT TEKUANYIN."

And,

"HEY I'M HERE TO TELL YA
THAT TEA IS HERE TO SPELL YA
SO WHEN YOU'RE TRIED AND TROUBLED
REACH FOR THAT TEKUANYIN."

And then, at the bottom of this pile was this sobering piece by Walt Whitman.

> I EXIST AS I AM,
> THAT IS ENOUGH.
> IF NO OTHER IN THE WORLD BE AWARE
> I SIT CONTENT.
> AND IF EACH AND ALL BE AWARE,
> I SIT CONTENT.
> ONE WORLD IS AWARE
> AND BY FAR THE LARGEST TO ME,
> AND THAT IS MYSELF.
> AND WHETHER I COME TO MY OWN TODAY
> OR IN TEN THOUSAND OR TEN MILLION YEARS,
> I CAN CHEERFULLY TAKE IT NOW
> OR WITH EQUAL CHEERFULNESS
> I CAN WAIT.

As I leafed through the box, it looked like Michael may have been organizing his files around the intention of writing a book because I found this list.

CHAPTER TITLES

I'LL TAKE MY MICHAEL O'DONNELL WITHOUT ANY TEA IN HIM THIS MORNING, THANK YOU!

HIGHLY TRANSFIGURED REVERSALS RATHER LATE IN THE DAY

THE CIRCUMVENTING PROSTHESES OF THE I CHING

REFINED TEAS REFINE US

TEA DATA IS FINITE, THE TEA EXPERIENCE IS NOT

THAT COUNTRY TO THE RIGHT OF IRELAND

33

HOMILY GRITS FOR THE MILL

TEA AND OPIUM PAIRING

THE QUESTION NO ONE'S ASKING: WOULD MY
HEALTH IMPROVE IF I WERE TO STOP DRINKING TEA?

WHY GONE: GAIWAN

GONG FU, FU GONE, WHERE'S MY FU, FREDDIE?

BACK TO THE SIXTIES (TURNING 60 AND GOING BACK
TO THE GREEN TEAS THAT NEED TO BE BREWED AT 60
DEGREES CELSIUS). Chapter might read: BACK TO THE
SIXTIES or SEX, DRUGS AND........FOLK MUSIC.

TEA: AN EXPLODED VIEW

Reading these titles, this humor, it was as if he were
sitting right here next to me.

Michael was always permitted a few idiosyncrasies by
those that loved him. They were more endearments really as
his "tea fried brain" often tipped the scales into an affected
pathology all his own.

Over a year ago, he had called and said he'd made
arrangements for a two week retreat up the road at the
monastery. He wanted to know if I'd be willing to meet him
at the Oak Grove when it ended, say at noon, and hang out
for a day or two. I said sure. Although I had trepidations
about spending so long a time with him, I didn't have to
think about it long to respond so quickly over the phone. I
hadn't seen Michael for a while. I also felt something was up.

There was a kind of tough love attitude I assumed
with him at times when I felt he was losing ground,
backsliding into his alcoholism as I felt he was now. I often
regretted how harsh I was. It was how I was with myself,
inclined toward asceticism. He hated what I had to say but

34

always listened. What he ended up doing with my "sug-gestions," my "directives," I've not a clue. There was a self-imposed limit to my "cross examinations," a governor. My love for Michael, my compassion, prevented me from being merciless.

We'd have fun at times, in our conversations, getting silly and superfluous. We thought alike on some things, found humor everywhere. There were places I did not tread, however, his childhood in the projects of South Boston was one.

We'd tease each other, nudge each toward growth but as we aged there was a chasm that widened between his desire for truth and my own.

IV

So, as noon approached on that day in October, I began to listen for the sound of a car engine coming down the river road. In the thin desert air cars were easy to hear from great distances. The low, muffled hum of shifting gears reverberated off the canyon walls. Michael's car was an exception though because its engine was so small and quiet, having only two cylinders, that I often saw it before I heard it and such was the case now as a glint of sun reflected off the tin roof and the unmistakable profile of his funny little Citroen Deux Chevaux. It was the perfect vehicle for his eccentric nature.

For being such a light car, the Citroen kicked up a fair amount of dust as it bounced and barreled down the road. The brown clouds of dirt passed through the trees and out over the river startling a herd of mallards that took off up river.

I left my chair and walked up the road to meet him.

Michael pulled in right in front of my car, opened his door, fiddled about, rummaging around inside the cab a bit and got out carrying a picnic basket and the driver's seat of his car.

"Michael!" We hugged.

"Franklin, you old stove."

Michael had the kind of smile and open face that immediately disarmed people and put them at ease. Even from a guy's perspective, he was a handsome man with his ruddy, Irish complexion and sandy blond hair but right now he looked tired, weary. I put my hand on his back.

"It's good to see you, Michael. How was your retreat?"

36

"It was good, productive. There weren't many people there so I felt like I had the whole place to myself. I'll share more about it later. Have you been here for a while? Are you ready for some tea?"

"Drove in yesterday." I said. "Needed a little quiet time of my own and yes, I'd love some tea. Thank you. Will you make the one you told me about, where we're going to get silly and irrelevant?"

"Irreverent too. Yes." he said.

"The other day you mentioned having had an epiphany with this tea. Explain."

"Well, look at the word epiphany, break it down." he said. "Epi means over, above or on top of and phany, fanny, is your butt. So, put it together. The experiences one has with this particular tea occur just above the butt, right here." He swivels from his hip, swings his arm around behind him, turns around, so I can see what he was doing and pressed his fingers to his lower back at about L4-5, the lumbar vertebrae.

Michael looked at me to see if I got it. I did.

"The Chinese call it the doorway of life" I offered, "and you've already had some of this tea haven't you?"

He smiled. "Another way to explain "epiphany" in this sense is what some women describe as "long, deep, rolling orgasms" where there is this sensation of opening and dropping, opening and dropping again and opening and dropping yet again so that you end up landing deep in your body onto that pelvic floor place you're always exclaiming about. You have a profound feeling of satisfaction and of being met. And then, as luck would have it, you get to hang out in that afterglow with your partner where another kind of tender "love making" unfolds. It's a lot like that space you describe where there is another, very different kind of tea ritual that begins long after your cup is empty."

Michael bent over and took hold of his picnic basket and car seat. He put his "beach chair" next to the two chairs I'd put out. We then headed over to the oaks and sat right down on the ground as we have done many times before.

"May I?" he asks.

"Yes, of course go ahead. It's still got some butane left in it. Here's some matches."

He pours water into my saucepan and when the water's ready he throws in some loose Puer and lets it boil.

We sat in silence for a couple of minutes till the tea was cooked. He poured the brew through a gourd strainer and served us up a cup. As he handed me one he added, "I hope you'll forgive me but I haven't any linens, coasters or cucumber sandwiches."

"None needed, mon ami."

We got up from the ground, strolled over to the chairs on the bluff and sat down.

I raised my cup and poured a little of the tea onto the ground.

Michael and I looked at each other, raised our cups to each other in a Namaste sort of a way and clinked them together.

"Slainte Gaelach." Michael said.

"L'chei-im," I retorted.

We took a sip of the tea at the same time and were silent again, this time for about five minutes.

"This is intense, Michael."

"Intense tea for intense people, Senor."

"This has got a full entry, mid-palette, finish. It engages my entire sensorium. That was a lot of leaf by the by, my captain. There's dried apricot here, in the back....dried plum, oak bark, bitter-sweet chocolate, a sort of a blond Virginia tobacco, old leather and then there's all the regular Pu-erh stuff: woody, earthy, elemental. Sweet, thick and gritty. Something reminds me of coffee here too."

"Yes, my Japanese friends call it "Thick Tea." Michael says.

We took another slug, another dip.

A few moments of silence passed as we contemplated the tea.

"So, your retreat?" I began.

"I could feel you praying for me. Your face would pop into my head from time to time. You were praying in the middle of the night too, weren't you?"

38

"I was indeed, Michael, but I'm sure there were a lot of people thinking of you, wishing you well, holding you in their hearts."

"No, this was different. It wasn't intercessory. It was different, a different quality, a different tone. It was.........it felt like..........it felt like I was floating.........floating in safety.........and love."

Michael bowed his head. A sadness broke out across the river and for a moment, it seemed, the birds were stilled. I saw tears dropping from his eyes, put my hand on his back and let him be.

"Thanks" he said heaving a sigh. "You're right. This stuff's pretty strong. I thought it might bring me to the point of one of your epiphanies."

"Looks like you're having one now, Michael. What's going on?"

"It was intense, the retreat. There weren't any distractions. I didn't bring any alcohol so I had to take a long hard look at myself. I felt real fragile and vulnerable and everything pushed my buttons. I kept on thinking of that woman you told me about who was so terrified by the silence and vast open spaces there that she fled the place on a road grader. I felt like running away too."

"But you didn't, Michael. You're probably real depleted too, aren't you? Do you still do yourself to help you sleep?

"Not every night." he said without looking at me.

"Does it work?"

"Not all the time. I wake up at 3 or so feeling groggy."

"You feel groggy 'cause you're hung over!" I said.

"How do you mean? I didn't have any wine or..."

"I mean that by depleting your vital life force like that, your chi, it'll make you feel sluggish when you wake and, as a result, you'll feel exhausted for a while until your chi replenishes itself. There are other types of hangovers besides those caused by alcohol."

"I can't wait around all day for my chi to replenish itself. I've got to get going in the morning." he said forcefully, defensively.

"So you make yourself a strong cup of tea in the morning?"

"Yes."

"And you make yourself another strong cup in the afternoon when you get that "sinking feeling"?"

"Yes."

"And then when you feel too hyper and irritable from the tea you have a glass of wine to calm you down, maybe several glasses? And then you smoke pot on top of all of this, right? This is not good, Michael. No wonder you look so run down."

I look out across the river to try to figure out what to say next. Michael follows my gaze, relieved for a moment that the conversation has shifted away from him and out over the river.

A wild turkey glides up into the empty branches of a Chinese elm across the river. It must have had a four foot wing spread. It was the largest bird in the canyon at this time of year.

"I've never seen a turkey up in a tree before," Michael said hoping to change the subject.

"Neither have I," I responded. "Maybe his tribe chose him to get up there and watch for predators, for eagles."

"You mean like they drew lots or something?"

"In their own turkey way, maybe. Why don't you cut back on the black tea and go to green? Used to be, that's all you drank. Why don't you explore the Japanese green teas? They're more meaty, beefy, substantial."

"Easier said than done," he said. "They all taste like a cross between kelp and fescue to me."

"Then cut back on the blacks, man! Make less for yourself. Use smaller gaiwans. Are you still going to AA?"

"No."

"Yoga?" I continued.

"Why should I do yoga when there's pain meds?"

"I think all the wine and pot has compromised your palate. Why else would you drink that frostbitten Nilgiri stuff? The leaf is dead on the bush before it's even harvested."

40

I turn straight at Michael and say, "You're not dead!"

Michael holds my gaze and says, "I drink it because I like the taste and you know about frost teas."

"The Japanese teas are bright, lively, nutritious. They'd be a perfect transitional tea for you. There's also some sort of an aesthetic liveliness that comes through her, those Japanese teas, which I've yet to explain. They'd cheer you up. What's going on in your personal life that finds you so caught up in this destructive cycle again?"

Silence.

"There's too much going on in your body right now, Michael. It's confused. You're sending it too many mixed signals, too many messages. It's a vicious cycle, Mick. You drink alcohol to calm yourself down, to get to sleep, after too much tea. Then you wake up with a hangover and to deal with the hangover you start drinking tea. I hope you're not taking any prescription medicines too."

Silence.

"So what should I do?"

"I'm telling you to cut back on the caffeine. Cut back on everything. Don't you meditate anymore?"

"Nope!"

"What about taking all your heart ache and turning it into a spiritual practice all its own, all your own? The flip side of addiction is spirituality. You told me that from one of your AA meetings."

He looked puzzled. "How do I do that?"

"You do what your constitution, your construction, affords you to do. You go where your brain chemistry leads you. If you're depressed, you go there, watch it, move through it, let it affect you, open to it, discern its message. Your spiritual practice can be one that your body is already in place to do. Accomplish that which your body leads you to. Just sit..........and track your stuff. Follow the warmth of the tea down into your belly and hang out there for a while. What is it you like about this tea?"

"The sludge at the bottom of the cup."

We smile.

Michael's energy shifts and he begins of close down. It's getting too threatening for him, too uncomfortable, too close to home...at least for the moment.

"OK. I'll back off."

"How about we put a dollop of something in this. It is a little sour, I do admit." Michael suggests.

"No, I like my Pu-erh naked and uncorrupted, thank you, and I thought you said you didn't bring any alcohol?"

"One of the monks gave me some."

I heave a sigh and give in. "Alright. Tell you what. I'll taste some of yours. What do you have and isn't this called aiding and abetting?"

"You're thinking of "enabling." I can't believe you're going to join me in a cup of adulterated tea."

"I rather think of it as abuse and I'm not joining you. I'm tasting yours."

"Oh, get off it. What about the whole idea of "tea party?" Have you forgotten? You get way too serious about your tea, Frankie, too rigid, elitist. Lighten up. Here."

Michael leans forward in his chair and pulls a gorgeous leather and sterling silver flask from his back pocket.

"Isn't that a Dunhill....?"

"Yes," he responds

"Did one of the monks give you that, too?"

"He was cleaning out and this is his Glenlivet, a Scotch."

He pours a little into his Pu-erh and hands it to me.

I take a sip.

I was shocked! It was good.

"This is still a little sour, Michael. You've over brewed it a little for my tastes but I see what you mean. Here, let's just take this another step further. Try some of this. Luo han guo, Monk's Fruit. It's a Chinese sweetener."

"You're kidding. That's what it's called? How appropriate. Two "monk-eys" on a river dipping....."

"Glenlivet and Luo Han Guo, the new milk and sugar," I say.

"Just getting into that party mood, Mick. Here. Try some," and I dip a bamboo tea spatula into the yellow powder, put a tiny amount on the end and put it right into Michael's mouth.

"Whoa! This is complex, changes every few seconds."

"I believe it and, yes, you're right. People forget that the very first time we heard about tea it was "packaged" right alongside another word and that other word was "PARTY." "TEA PARTY." They came as one unit and thus shall they be ever bound, intertwined in love and devotion, joyousness and fellowship."

"Amen!"

"A-women!"

"More Scotch?"

"No thanks."

"Oh, pooh!"

"What?'

"I feel a seizure coming on."

"I'll get the tape recorder, but don't expect me to keep up with you, Michael."

Michael entered states of a different order than the ones that consumed me. Some of them were of great concern because of their effects on his health. They were no less powerful and profound he would argue. To the many people he had alienated, who thought that they were no more than drunken rantings scribbled down after a few drinks, I, here in this book, lay bare before you the heart of a troubled and compassionate soul for all to see. For me he was a visionary, lightly salted or slightly altered by the touch of tea. So here is another kind of possession, of seizure, when our muses step into the light to work their magical resplendencies.

Michael gets up from his chair and takes off. The Oak Grove becomes Saint Camellia's Church of the First Infusion, the oaks themselves, his congregants.

"The reading today is from the Gospel according to The Band, from their hymn "Up On Cripple Creek," written by Robbie Robertson.

"Now there's one thing in the whole wide world
I sure would like to see,
That's when that little love of mine
Dips her doughnut in my tea.

"Up on Cripple Creek she sends me
If I spring a leak she mends me,
I don't have to speak, she defends me
A drunkard's dream if I ever did see one."

"My brothers and sisters, this is not going to be a
dainty dissertation for the crumpet crowd because if you do
not know how to make a cup of tea for yourselves by now
then the Lord have mercy on your soul.

"I've been to your homes and I have observed how
some of you make tea and yes, I'm looking at you, Miriam.
Putting a tea bag in a mug of tap water and putting it in the
microwave with some Haagen Dazs Honey Vanilla ice cream
is not acceptable. And you, Philbert, boasting that there's no
mess to clean up when you make tea in a Cuisinart is out-
rageous. Sit up straight now, and where the hell'd you get
that tie?

"People, what you do in the privacy of your own
homes is your business but be forewarned, sooner or later
your deceitful tricks will catch up with you.

"My friends, one of the issues I labored with in writing
these homilies was how to use expletives in a religious context. For example, last week, a member of the congregation
came up to me after the service and said, "Padre, sometimes
I don't care about being whisked away into the land of the
Celestial Immortals by some spectacular tasting Oolong! I
just want a fucking cup of tea!"

"My son," I replied, "if we defile tea, as the English do,
then we become like them. When you desecrate tea with
milk and sugar it ceases to be tea and becomes a food group.
However, when we Irish splash a little whiskey into our tea it
is magically transformed into a golden elixir of immortality.
Dwell on that, my son!

"My friends, let it be known unto you that the English have never been known for their sophisticated palates. Their choice of tea is evidence of this. Why the world continues to attribute their ritual around the tea-like substance they wash their food down with to be the pinnacle of Western protocol and etiquette is a mystery to me.

"What I am saying then, is that what the English drink is not tea at all but a botanical beverage product. A botanical beverage product that cannot be improved no matter how much milk and sugar you put into it, no matter how many royal emblems and insignias are printed on their tins, no matter how elegant the caddy or exotic the tea.

"My friends! Please! Remember this! The English did not discover tea! The English did not invent tea or teatime! Tea does not grow in England! Silver teapots and fine porcelain are not products of the English imagination! These are all Chinese things. Even the very term, English tea is an oxymoron to some of us! So what was England's contribution to the world of tea?"

"Opium!" I yell. "And what have the Irish contributed to tea, Padre?" I continue.

"Colorful language!" he quips but his breathing had become labored.

"Are we going to have another tea and opium pairing class after Sunday School today, Father?" I inquired.

Michael paused. His face went white and he collapsed onto the ground. I thrust myself out of my chair, knelt beside him to feel his pulse and watch his respirations. Satisfied, I stood up, went over to my van and returned with a cotton throw to cover him with. I brought my chair over to where he was, sat back down and watched him.

Because of how he was laying, I could see the pulse on his right wrist throbbing in the sun. I studied it for quite some time, mindless amusement I suppose, but after a while I noticed it had begun to skip a few beats.

"Damn," I thought and looked out at the water.

V

BCH

You couldn't get on to the eighth floor of Dowling Building at Boston City Hospital (BCH) without donning a surgical cap, gown and booties. This is where I saw Michael for the first time, sitting on a bench in the coffee room, reading my copy of the "I Ching," the grey one, and smoking a cigarette. His green cloth wrap-around gown had come undone and I noticed he'd removed his clerical collar, a cheap little piece of white plastic, and placed it in the chest pocket of his black clerical shirt where it stuck out. I don't think he'd slept for several days. A nurse came in, motioned to him and he was gone. Over the months, I watched Michael comfort friends and families from his congregation. They came up on elevators from the Emergency Room on the ground floor. Parents often accompanied their kids, who were stretched out on gurneys, up to this little hallway. At this point, we'd roll the gurneys onto the surgical floor and the parents would go back down to the waiting rooms at ground level.

Michael was a local parish priest at the Gate of Heaven Catholic Church on East 4th Street in "Southie." What struck me most about Michael, however, was that he was also ministering, tending, to the non-Catholic parents and kids that came in from other parts of the city, Roxbury mostly.

It was the early 1970's and the City of Boston was court ordered to desegregate their schools. Children of African-American descent were bused into the Irish Catholic neighborhoods of Southie, South Boston, and Irish Catholic kids were bused into black neighborhoods. It was a disaster. Racial violence erupted across the city. The worst incidents were in Southie. State troopers were stationed at South Boston High for three years and Boston City Hospital was in the middle of it all.

I was an operating room technician or "scrub tech," which is the person that hands all the instruments to the surgeons during various procedures. They also called us "scrub nurses" but we were not RNs. Although my experiences as a medical corpsman in the Navy during the late sixties and early seventies qualified me for this position, it did not prepare me for the kind of heartless brutality I was witnessing.

From time to time, I'd also see Michael at Fiona's Apoco-Fukien-Lyptic House of Tea where I'd go after work for a beer or two with some of the nurses. That's right, a teashop with a liquor license right there on Harrison Avenue.

One time Michael was at a small table with a couple of other priests and two law enforcement officers. I sat down at a big table with the nurses just as Michael's table was breaking up. We all looked over at them as they left but Michael stayed behind. He still looked exhausted and quite disheveled on top of that. One of the nurses called out to him. He looked over, got up from his table with a teapot in one hand and a cup and saucer in the other and joined us. All the nurses greeted him with "Father' and Michael, on his part, acknowledged them all by name.

As I was new at "City," Mary Kelly introduced us. Michael saw that I was studying his cup and teapot because I'd never seen anything like it at Fiona's before. It was Spode China, from England, and hand painted.

"It's mine." He said. "They keep it here for me."

"What was that all about?" Mary inquired as she nodded over at where Michael had been sitting. Michael said nothing.

"You from Southie, Frank?" Michael asked me.

"Quincy." I said.

"Part of the "White Flight?"

"Nope."

"Where are you living now?" Michael asked.

47

"Cambridge." I said.

"Oh, do you know Father...."

"I'm not Catholic."

"With a name like Murphy you're not Catholic? Are you a left handed Irishman then?"

It was an obscure Irish euphemism. No one at the table knew what Michael was referring to but everyone still watched to see how I'd answer.

"Yes, sir, I'm left handed," I said with a smile.

Michael exploded with an absolutely delightful laugh and slapped me on the back. I truly believe he expected me not to know what he meant. It meant I was Protestant.

I really didn't want to get into the whole thing so I changed the subject.

"I see you flipping through the pages of that "I Ching" there in the coffee room from time to time. What do you think?"

"Is that yours? Well, I'll tell you what I think. I was so impressed with it that I went over to that Cambridge of yours the other day and bought a copy."

"I hope that wasn't parish money you used to buy that book with, Father," one of the nurses joked.

Everyone laughed and whatever tension there was broke as the waitress came by with five bottles of stout.

"More tea, Father?" the waitress asked.

Michael handed her the teapot and off she went.

"What kind of tea are you drinking, Michael?" I asked.

"A green tea. Gunpowder. Temple of Heaven. I like the name. It reminds me of my church, Gate of Heaven. Why do you ask? Are you a tea enthusiast?"

Before I could answer the waitress returned with Michael's teapot and proceeded to pour him a cup but the fragrance that whirled up from the surface of that steaming concoction was not of tea alone and I recognized the high evaporative esters of an alcoholic beverage.

A police officer appeared at the door of the tearoom. "Father!" he called out and Michael was off. No sooner had he risen from the table than his finely crafted porcelain tea service was whisked away by the same waitress that had placed it there.

After two years doing trauma at "City" or "BCH," I'd burned out, left New England and moved to New Mexico.

Over the years, I read about the sexual abuse scandals that erupted within the Catholic Church in Boston in the '90's. I'd also been hearing about it from some of the nurses I kept in touch with. They told me that Michael had become an outspoken advocate for the many victims of sexual abuse in his archdiocese and had even helped them organize. He had become a thorn in the side of the archdiocese. So when Michael was interviewed by the Boston Globe for one of their articles exposing these pedophile priests, Michael made a couple of statements that the church asked him to retract. He refused.

The church was acutely aware of how beloved Michael was in both the Irish Catholic and African-American communities, so, as a consequence, they asked him to leave for a period of time, to get some help with his drinking and to reflect on his future with the church. And the best place to do that was at a place called The Servants of the Paraclete, founded, interestingly, by another priest from Boston, a Fr. Gerald Fitzgerald. Its location was in the Jemez Mountains of northern New Mexico and was full of alcoholic as well as, unfortunately for Michael, pedophile priests.

In 2010, at the Monastery of Christ in the Desert, just up the road, we met again.

We were both staying at the guest facility and happened to be in the "common room" at the same time. This was a large room immediately adjacent to the guest area but in a building by itself. It had a kitchen, library, lavatory and a fireplace. There was a small fire there now.

I was in the process of posting a sign on the glass door when Michael came over from the kitchen area to take a look and started laughing. The sign read "There will be no more go kart races in the chapel after vespers."

Of all the people I worked with on the eighth floor of Dowling Building 35 years ago, I can picture every single face. When you're watching people die from gunshot wounds, people cut open with their internal organs exposed, the people that you depend on to get you something immediately imprint themselves into your psyches for the rest of your life. Michael was no different. He was one of the gang. I recognized him immediately.

"Michael O'Donnell! Dowling 8. Boston City Hospital. 1973."

"Oh, wow," he said. He stared at me, studying my face but nothing registered.

"Would you like a cup of tea?"

"Yes, I would. Thank you. What brings you to this place now, Michael? Do you live in the area?"

"Santa Fe. And you? What brings you here?"

"I live in Santa Fe, too, and I've been coming here since the late 70's, but I'm not Catholic."

"What's the pull then?"

"History and the beauty. I used to come here with my late wife. I don't go to the services much anymore. Just take long walks down the road."

"Your first wife was Catholic then?"

"Jewish."

Michael paused.

The water was boiling. He'd already put some tea into a tea ball, hooked it over the edge of the pot and poured the water in. The care he put into the task before him was evident and for a moment I thought I noticed him make the sign of the cross over the leaves as they brewed.

"Do you dot your "i's" and cross your teas, Michael?"

He smiled. "Do you go to the monastery for retreats anymore, Frank? Frank?"

Michael had wakened from his "nap."

"Where were you?"

"Right here, brother. Right here talking with you. Are you alright?" I asked.

"I'm ready for some more tea and something to eat."

50

VI

PUER IS NOT FROM PUER-TO RICO

I gave Michael a choice between the last of a veggie mix or a can of pork and beans. He chose the latter, popped the lid and devoured it, cold, right out of the can using one of those Swiss Army knives with the spoon.

"Would you like some more then?" I asked.

"Later maybe. Are you going to make some tea?"

"A Dian Hong." I replied.

"Oh, good. Make it the way you make it for yourself. I won't interrupt you."

"There's no wind right now. I'll bring everything over here." I offered.

"Thanks."

"Feeling better?" I asked.

"Yah."

I got up from my chair, walked back into the trees, wrapped up all the porcelain in white terrycloth, bar towels really, put it all in the canvas bag (the LL Bean Boat and Tote one), brought it over and set it all up again. Except this time, I pulled a teapot out from the bottom, unwrapped it and placed it in the dirt at his feet. The dirt wasn't the same soft, dark, composted humus that was under the oaks but a fine, powdered clay. If you blew on it, it would puff up into your face. Many a time, a rogue wind would pop up over the cliff edge as I was imbibing and cover the surface of my tea with a fine silt. I drank it anyway. It was a blessing. "Drink this!" Pachamama said.

It was the same dynamic with a dream I had about a Yixing teapot. The point of the dream was not to cure the pot as one is advised to do with Yixing ware, to "cook" the pot in a saucepan with the tea you'd be using it for. The point was to take into my body all of the mineral essences of the pot itself, even if that meant the tea would taste like clay for a while. Even if, sometime down the road, I broke the pot, the dream advised me to brew my tea right along with the broken fragments. There was some sort of, let's call it energy work, energy medicine, that would utilize these minerals from China in my body. When I was "counseled" to "Use the Pot!" say during the more challenging moments in my life, there would always come insights, clarity, into that situation.

The teapot I'd just unwrapped, however, was not Yixing but porcelain and had a thick white enameled finish. Painted upon it were dark red peonies. It was stunning. I hadn't used it before."

"Exquisite!" Michael blurted. "Looks like we'll be up for a while this evening, Franklin."

The water came to a boil quickly and I placed a goodly mound of the Dian Hong's golden tips into the bottom of the pot with a bamboo spoon. I had the feeling the pot was taking the leaves out of the spoon for me.

"I've had that feeling before, too," Michael offered.

Sometimes when you're sharing, creating ritual space with another person, there are moments when you enter states of receptivity so magical that everyone's picking up, sensing, everything. Michael could be incredibly psychic when he wanted to be, when he felt safe, let's say.

Michael shuffled about in his chair a bit and sat up.

I lifted the pan off the stove and poured the boiling water into the pot. I'd misjudged its capacity. There was not enough water to fill it.

As the leaves brewed, I offered simple prayers of gratefulness,...........and love.

I held my palm over the pot and drew my energy, my chi, up from my belly, down my arm and out through my palm into the tea. I hadn't put the lid on so I watched, and felt the hot steam engulf my whole hand. There was first the sensation that the steam helped to open the pores in my skin and then there was the feeling that the tea was pulling my chi out of my palm, into itself. When that sensation subsided, when the tea had stopped "pulling on me," I withdrew my hand and dried it with one of the towels. At that moment, Michael leaned forward and emptied the rest of the scotch

52

into the mix, put the lid on and started giggling. I was so shocked I didn't know what to do.

Michael sees my dismay, my confusion. I give in.

"Oh, what the heck," I said out loud. "It might be fun."

"Now you're talking!" Michael chimed.

The Dian Hongs were a versatile and forgiving clan and could withstand most adulterants. In my exuberance, I often over-brewed the leaves, making a syrupy elixir that some said catapulted them into their next incarnation. Some even claimed it incinerated all of their karmic destiny. Most, however, particularly women friends, preferred the second infusion.

It was with the Dian Hongs, the Yunnan Reds or Yunnan Royal Golds, that I had had most of my more unusual experiences and insights into tea so this was going to be interesting.

Michael and I both heard the monastery bell ring, distant and muffled but distinct.

"Tea's ready." Michael was excited, animated.

He reached into his picnic basket and extracted two 14 ounce French jam jars with red plastic covers. He ripped the lids off and handed them to me. He was all anxious, poised on the threshold of launching into something.

"Oh, God. Here we go," I mumbled.

And to the brim I filled both of these Pyrex tumblers. I handed one to Mike and the other I held up to the light, but as the Scotch was the same dark amber as the tea, I saw nothing different. I brought the glass to my nose and the fragrance of the alcohol went straight into my brain stem.

I saw that Mike had taken quite a gulp. "Wow, this is wonderful," he said. "Is there more?"

I took a sip and was, well, impressed.....again.

The sun was low in the west and reflected off the water with such intensity that we put vizored caps on. The blinding light shot up into the oaks, illuminating the leaves from underneath and filling the grove with a strange, iridescent glow.

53

"Interesting light there, que no?" Michael commented.

"Yes. Enchanting, really. Mesmerizing. It feels like the grasses and the leaves are emitting their own light."

"I think you're emitting your own light right now, Mr. Murphy."

I looked over at him and smiled.

"Could be. Could be."

Then Michael started in.

"People that think distilled water tastes flat don't like it 'cause it reminds them of their own dull and boring lives."

"Where did that come from? How did you get from...."

"The water. It jumped right out of the river like a trout, clear up into the air and then splashed back down."

"Michael, pretty soon, I may not be able to track you, all that you say, but yes..."

He went on.

"It's the same with fresh water. Well, what the hell is that? Everyone in the tea industry talks about using fresh water for tea but no one explains what they mean by it. They assume that you know already when, in fact, they themselves do not know. For example, my question here is, is fresh water fresh when it comes out of your tap or is it fresh long before it comes out of your tap, up at the water treatment plant where chlorine and fluoride are added to it? Is it fresh when it fills the reservoirs as snowmelt or bubbles up into them from underground springs? Is it fresh when your pump pulls it up from beneath the ground or is it fresh when it falls as snow in the mountains or as rain in town? Is it fresh when it evaporates from the oceans to form clouds? Is bottled water fresh when you buy it or fresher when it's bottled at the source?"

"You've been thinking about this. You're moving too fast for me, Miguel."

"No faster than the river, my friend. Look at it now."

It had risen again. There'd been another release. I didn't notice it because it was a lot quieter. There's a point where it gets so high, that all the boulders are underwater

54

and the river flows silently through the canyon, seemingly unobstructed.

I saw that Michael's glass was nearly empty. I was saddened but I had no judgment about it really. He was just rushing on ahead to things that he'd been obsessing about so I poured him another. The sun dropped below the western rim of the canyon and we were, once again, in shade. The whole canyon softened, there was a profound sense of relief and our bodies resumed their relaxed and care free temperament. We removed our caps, took a deep breath and had another slug of this "golden elixir of immortality."

Even the birds, that yesterday came alive in the warmth and brilliance of the morning light, soared and darted about the river catching flies with playful, dramatic maneuverings. These were the swallows, las golondrinas, who lived in mudded nests high along the canyon walls.

I slipped into a playful mood and threw Michael a curve ball. "Michael, don't you think it was the mud nests, the houses of the swallows with their vigas and latias that inspired the ancient Celtic people to build their adobes houses in Choco Canyon (Chaco Culture National Historic Park, NM)?"

He didn't lose a step.

"We learned that in elementary school, Franco. The cool thing is that if you kick around long enough in the trailings of the open pit chocolate mines there, you can still find enough chocolate to make yourself some brownies. Course, by the time we (the Celts, the Irish) sold the place to the Pueblo People all the chocolate had been played out and they changed the name to Chaco Canyon (See: New Mexi-cocoa) and they never mention the Celts. By the by, I wanted to ask you about that chapter title you'd been kicking around, the one for the Puer section."

I looked as attentive as I could but really just wanted to be zooming about with the birds, left alone.

He continued.

"I can understand you wanting to use the other spelling but don't you think that "The Pre-Puer Pee and the Post-Puer Poop" is a little PUER-ile for a chapter title in a tea

55

book? I know that the very thought of preparing Puer stimulates peristalsis but..."

"No book about tea would be complete without a chapter on urination." I add. "So rather than discuss the entire alimentary system, I'll just call it "Passing Water.""

"Thank goodness." He said with a smirk.

"How about the issue of what Jung called the puer aeturnus complex?" I flash.

"Which is...?"

"The Peter Pan thing, about men who don't want to grow up. Do you think that Puer might cure people of that?"

"How might it do that?"

"By accelerating the maturation process. It accelerates everything else."

"The same way caffeine is said to accelerate the reproduction of cellular abnormalities?" Michael added.

"Sort of but would it not also accelerate the reproduction of normal, healthy cells, even a desire to grow, mature?"

"Never thought of it like that before."

"What was that conversation you had with that lady about Pooh Bear?" I asked.

"A parent asked me if there were any relationship between Pu-er and Pu-bear.

"Yes, I told her. A. A. Milne came up with the idea for his books while sipping Pu-er in China and, of course, seeing all the adorable pandas in the zoos there."

Silence.

Still silence.

"And Yogi Bear?" I asked.

"He's from India."

"Did you ever think any more about creating that tea menu for the different liturgical hours of the day: a black tea for Lauds, a white for Vespers and all that? What did you come up with for Mass?"

"Well, that's the rub isn't it, the Mass. History will eventually show that when Jesus married Mary Magdalene at that wedding in Cana, and he performed his first miracle, and who wouldn't be able to toss a miracle or two taking a gorgeous, red haired, firebrand from Northern Ireland as a wife? I'd toss a miracle or two, myself. Want one now?"

"Later," I said.

"What, a wife or a miracle?"

"Back on point, Michael. The point being..." and I make 'get on with it' gestures with my hands.

"The point being that the Greek, Aramaic and Chinese characters for tea are all identical, suggesting that Christ did not turn water into wine to impress his beautiful wife, he turned water into tea. And that, similarly, the bush Moses saw drinking without consuming itself on Mount Sinai was none other than a tea bush. It is a profound tragedy indeed that the Catholic Church voted to disregard these facts because it was easier to subdue, pacify and control the masses with wine rather than to empower them with tea. I think that if the church had stayed with tea they wouldn't be in the mess they're in today."

"So then when did the church switch over to using wine in the Mass rather than tea?" I asked.

"That was later...at a party."

"Well, you know what the Bible says," I add. "The goddess of tea, Thea, enters a room anytime two or more people gather in her name. I believe that's from Ephesians."

"And if forty or more people gather in her name?" Michael asks.

"She brings her husband."

"Who is...?"

"Hyperion. By the way, why doesn't your Christian god have a mate? Everybody else does."

"Got me there." Michael responds.

A coyote trots through the campsite. We note "coyote" and gaze back out at the river.

"So, to review, Thea is a deity from which all light proceeds. Thea married Hyperion, the Titan-god of light, and bore him three bright, light bearing children--Helios the Sun, Eos the Dawn, and Selene the Moon."

"Will we be blinded by all these light bearing gods, Frank, right here at the river?"

"Only for a few moments, Michael. But then with everything so lit up all around you, you may see things you hadn't noticed before, and you're beginning to slur your words."

"So?"

"I'd appreciate it if you would enunciate better because I don't want to have to recreate your sloppy diction in this book. It's too much work."

"You don't have to let your readers know I'm drunk." Michael offered.

"That'll work. A friend asked me once why I needed to make the characters in my book drunk in order for them to say certain outlandish things, why I needed the excuse of drunkenness?"

"And?"

"She was a former alcoholic so found issue with it. I said that she had a point and let it go. I'm gonna jump in the river, Mister Mike."

"A little cold for that, isn't it? It's getting dark!"

"Where?"

"It's that Norwegian blood of yours, isn't it? I'm going to stroll down the road then. See you in a bit."

"K."

I'd finished about half my drink. I was amazed at how good it tasted, just like the scotch and Pu-erh earlier.

I lumbered up out of my chair feeling heavier than usual and started to make my way along the cliff till I found the way down.

At the bottom, I had to pass through a dense willow thicket to get to the water but once out on the warm sand, I stripped down to my skivvies and waded out. With each step, I'd sink down into mud sometimes up to my knees. I bent over and cupped water into my face and over my head. It was brisk. I never could relate to that tea term. For me "brisk" meant a naked dip in the North Atlantic in April. WHOA!

I laid down in the water on my tummy and looked up river feeling the force of the water flowing over my skin. If I didn't have my feet dug into the mud I would've been carried off. With my mouth underwater, my view was at eye level and I saw the river rising in front of me. I was basically looking "uphill" if you will, an interesting perspective being a foot or two below the level of the water as I watched it coming toward me from a couple of hundred feet ahead.

On hot summer days, when I was feeling my oat bran, I'd swim upriver against the current for the thrill of it.

After a while, I got up, sludged through the mud to the bank and sat down. The cold of the water had sobered me, grounded me and returned me to myself. Not that I'd strayed that far. It was fun being silly with Michael and all but I didn't like the way alcohol made me feel. For that matter, sometimes I didn't even like the way tea made me feel. If I made too strong a cup I'd be tense, angry and afraid. At these points it felt like tea taxed my endocrine system, the adrenals mainly, and my thyroid would get sore. I was a lightweight really. My life, my acute sensitivities made things interesting enough without having to deal with something in my body that either numbed my relationship with myself, with nature, or intensified it. When I saw Michael's chapter entitled "I'll Take My Michael O'Donnell Without Any Tea In It Today, Thank You," I could relate. I wish he felt the same way about the sauce.

The cold waters of the river had wakened me but there was a back reserve of awareness that came, I think, from the tea. I recalled a joke I heard years ago. "You never make someone that's intoxicated drink a lot of coffee because there's nothing worse than a wide awake drunk."

Regardless of this back reserve, the scotch had zapped my energy and I had yet to set up the tents.

So I waded back through the willows, clambered up the clay embankment and found Michael passed out on the ground. He was using the cushions of my chair as a mattress, crumpled up a jacket for a pillow and covering him was that thin cotton throw. I guess he either didn't bring any camping equipment or couldn't be bothered. Well, at least I wouldn't have to set up any tents. My bedroll under the oaks was where I had left it.

I also noticed that my glass was empty and so was the teapot.

I went to my van and grabbed an extra sleeping bag to cover him with. It was late October and going to get cold.

I knew that if didn't do something to help myself there might be a hangover waiting for me in the morning, so I drank a lot of water and swallowed an aspirin, a B-complex and a quercetin/bromelain tablet. Any residual hangover, a strong pot of Pu-erh would dispatch.

Michael was out for the evening so I sat up for a while.

It had been a long while since I'd spent any time at the monastery. My Ashkenazi wife was fascinated by the place, particularly the prayer life. When she died I continued to go but lost interest over time. It was always the staggering beauty of the canyon that appealed to me the most. It was where I communed. I'd go up for a retreat but spend most of the time out in the clay hills and canyon lands.

I remember sitting in the chapel one day during mass and realizing that there wasn't a single word I could relate to in the liturgy. All of a sudden, everything was so foreign, so discordant to my own personal experiences of the divine that I began to look at Catholicism not as a religion but as a pathology.

A line of James Hillman's popped into my head. "We've had a hundred years of psychotherapy and the world is getting worse."

Why stop there I thought. Can't we also say that we've had 3,000 years of organized religion and civilization is getting worse? The same may be said of science.

When an individual has his own experiences of the divine, Christianity can look absolutely bankrupt. It did for me anyway. And I think that's what people are beginning to discover for themselves, a certain vacuity in religions, the hollow words of empty men. There seems to be a movement back toward the spirituality that predates organized religions, a movement that bespeaks a return to the fertile ground from which all religions sprouted, shamanism.

Like in that poem earlier, all my life I had the sense that there was something else, something much more mysterious than what I was hearing in church. Still, I had to reject it all, distance myself from it, in order to evaluate it over time, on my own. That was when I was twelve. At 24, when I was at Boston City Hospital, things began to shift. I started seeing auras floating on the ceilings of the surgical theaters during frontal lobe brain procedures. Some of the auras where so bright they reflected off my surgical instruments. The odd thing was, it didn't surprise me.

VII

BACK TABAC

"I'm tired of living within the accepted confines of this stupid species." Michael O'Donnell

I woke to voices, raised my head and looked over to where Michael had crashed. He was laying there awake, obsessing, talking out loud.

I heaved a sigh. I'd been hesitant to spend this much time with him. My limit was usually two hours. So instead of letting him obsess all over me (we'd get to it eventually), I decided to change the subject before the subject presented itself. I got up, went over and sat down next to him. He'd already started drinking.

"Hey! Good morning, Mister Mick, how was your walk yesterday. See anything?"

"Usual stuff. Herd of penguins flew over. Pterodactyl swooped down and made off with one of your friend's steers, and those stupid ass jackalopes, lumbering about under the weight of their antlers, poor things, useless animal, really. Not good for much of anything in the long run except tourism. I remember reading that in the 1970's, the Forest Service tied bandanas around their necks as a sort of tracking device but a year later the kerchiefs ended up on all the coyotes. What a joke. As a way to remind the Forest Service just how stupid that idea was, there were all these wooden coyotes outside storefronts in Santa Fe with bandanas tied around their necks. That's where that comes from but you never saw anything about it in the papers."

"I did not know that." I said it with an appreciative smile then picked up his drink and held it up to his face. "Is this your eye-opener/hair of the dog thing?" I inquired.

"Just a split............Piper-Heidsieck. Want some?"

"No, thanks. I'm going to make tea, for the both of us. How long have you been awake?"

"Several hours. How can a culture that's been so brutal, so cruel, be so polite and have a highly refined aesthetic on top of that?"

"So you've been obsessing about the Japanese Tea Ceremony?"

"Frankie? You don't have to be a fucknician..."

"Fucknician, Michael?"

"You don't have to be a fucking technician to make yourself a cup of tea. I think the whole thing over-focuses on the ritual, the performance, and not on the tea. If Rikyu did truly say "The way of tea is nothing but this: First you boil the water, then you make the tea and then you drink it," then what went wrong here? Seems to me that he didn't take his wabi sabi stuff far enough into the ritual itself. I appreciate all the "crude, anonymous, indigenous Japanese and Korean" farm craft tea ware but think he should have gone further, or that someone else, later, should have, to have reduced the ritual to its fewest moving parts. The body movements are not wabi sabi. How the hostess sits is not wabi sabi. It makes my body uncomfortable watching the hostess be uncomfortable in theirs.

"The ceremony has nothing to do with the plant, the spirit of the plant or even saying thank you. It can even appear to exude a sort of dissonance that's hostile to the nature of tea. Tea doesn't present itself as being constrained and exacting.

"And sure, you can read about all the great intentions that Rikyu and many others had for the ceremony but they're a lot of lofty ideas and that's about it, someone's fanciful ideas of spirituality. It still remains an inordinately complicated performance. Needs a makeover for relevancy. You want wabi sabi? Throw some tea leaves in an open saucepan of boiling water. That's what I do.

"And I don't like Matcha. It's over manipulated, looks synthetic and tastes like dirt. Dreadful stuff!"

"Matcha's an acquired taste, Mister Michael. It grows on you."

"You mean like a wart?"

"No, I mean like Pu-erh. Now there's an acquired taste for you, que no?"

Silence.

"It's still beautiful ceremony isn't it, Michael?"

Still silence.

I continue:

"You banana head. Each of the world's dominant tea cultures: the Chinese, Japanese and English, have chosen to express their passion for tea in their own unique ways. It's as if the Japanese have elevated almost everything they do to ritual status. It is as it should be. Should not all of life be lived in ritual if we are truly grateful? A friend of mine once described the ceremony as choreographed calligraphy. I thought that was cool."

Silence. Then Michael went on.

"Then what's the insidious, undercurrent of elitism that pervades it and its people. It's its own very unique brand of affectation."

"All tea cultures are saturated with pretension, haughtiness, arrogance, don't you think? What's all this cynicism about, Michael? What's going on? Did something happen on your retreat you're not telling me?"

Silence.

I let it run and sat motionless. It was my intention to give Michael a lot of space, nurture it even if I could. I felt his struggle, searching for words, for feelings. His whole body shifted into pain. It was palpable. Tears rolled down his face and dropped on his shirt. And then there was a release.

The silence continued for quite a while. I gazed out over the river and waited. Birds flew about. A small dust devil came out over the river and I could see three different whirling patterns on the surface of the water as though the devil were itself composed of three different winds.

"Are you sleeping better these days, Mr. Frank?"

It was the first time Michael had inquired about how I was doing. I reached out and put my hand on his shoulder.

"I'm getting help from Dr. Zhou. Chinese herbs. Talk about something tasting like dirt. I'm also watching my tea intake. Doing deep breathing exercises when I wake in the middle of the night."

"Tell me that story again, about the breathing tree."

"That's a long story, Michael."

He looked over at me and smiled gently.

"I can pay attention now."

"Alright. It was the night my first wife died. Before she went to sleep, she wanted to take a med. that would help her to sleep but might also exacerbate her asthma. I read it on the syllabus and told her so. There were four of us there and we asked Aarone go in and "ask her angels" what to do. It would be all right, she said. Well, she died that night of asphyxiation and I carried that with me for 17 years, waking each night from sleep apnea at 3:33 AM, the moment of her death.

"Now here's the interesting part. Years before I even met Aarone, when I first got to New Mexico, I was very intrigued by an area of land on the Rio Grande north of Santa Fe near one of the Pueblos. I kept going there and exploring the place but couldn't figure out what it was about, why it seemed to be calling me. After a while, I forgot about it.

"Then, like I said, 17 years after Aarone passed, I was working on an estate and was chatting with one of the workmen there. He invited me over to his house for tea and told me how to get there. We set a date and I drove over. The entrance to his place was in this same region right along the Rio Grande. My friend comes out to greet me and immediately starts talking about this cottonwood tree that's there at the river's edge. He said that at two different times, he hosted a couple of shamans that were visiting the area, one from Central America and the other from South America and that when they got out of their cars they both noticed the energy of the tree immediately. My friend then asked me if I would like to go take a look. Sure I said, so we strolled over and when we got there he invited me to lie down in the exposed roots of this massive specimen. I laid down and closed my eyes and the tree, with one inhalation, took me into it and with another, the exhalation, breathed me out.

65

When I woke that night at 3:33 AM, I repeated the breath the way the tree had taught me, fell back to sleep and never suffered from sleep apnea again. I was, pun intended, blown away."

"Amazing. Thanks. But you're still waking in the middle of the night?" Michael inquired.

"Yes, but it's a different time, 2 AM, and I think it's related to my liver. I'll find out more at my next appointment. At least it's not that terror my body seizes up with in sleep apnea when I stop breathing altogether."

"Tell me about the herbs."

I kept going. Michael felt more in his body, more grounded, as though he'd come to terms with something.

"A lot of people complain about Chinese herbs. Some make you gag. I understand all that but then I have this resonance with all things Chinese, particularly plant substances. So when I take a shot of some strange elixir I can feel its effects as soon as it hits my tongue. It's a lot like the immediate shift I feel when I take a homeopathic remedy, when it's the right one. They're all real subtle energy medicines.

"I remember when my daughter, Kyrie, was about three months old. She had colic and was screaming wildly. There was nothing we could do to console her as she flailed about in our arms with this intense gastric pain. As parents, we were beside ourselves so we decided to try a homeo-pathic. We looked up a remedy and landed on Colocynthis. We popped four in her mouth and instantaneously she was asleep. I know, too, of a lot of people who either say that homeopathics don't work for them or that they think it's a lot of bull, placebos. I'll tell you one thing, the people that really see the dramatic and spontaneous healings are parents when they hit on the right remedy for their children."

"Are you thinking about going to see Doctor Zhou, Mike?"

"No, I was thinking that maybe alcohol's been sort of my ally plant, the "grain spirits" so to speak because it's been what's kept me alive all these years. On the other hand, I think it's been my spiritual path to the wrong address.

"When I was over in the Jemez there at the Servants of the Paraclete, we used to talk about it in group, that alcoholism wasn't curable. It was just something you managed. Pedophilia was the same thing. They used to have us say Mass several times a day as if that would do anything. I understood the rational but it didn't work. It had the reverse effect on me. Celebrating it so often like that made it fatuous, vapid. It was much more interesting, in private sessions, to talk about Joseph Campbell, M. Ester Harding, Erich Neumann, Mircea Eliade, all those Bollingen Press people.

"And then in through the front door walks the pedophile priest from the Boston Archdiocese that was the primary abuser, perpetrator, of all the kids that came to me with their heart breaking stories."

And here, Michael breaks down. He falls forward out of his chair onto his knees, then onto the ground and sobs.

Felt like the whole canyon filled with his pain.

"I'm consumed with rage," he continues "run at him and smash him in the face so hard I break his mandible and he spends the next few weeks with his jaw wired up eating out of a straw. They retired me after that one." He laughs.

"Celibacy's such a joke. It's a rare person who it works for, people who have a true calling for it, but homosexuality's rampant.

"Christ wasn't celibate. He was a rabbi. It would have been very unusual if he were not married. When the church instituted celibacy it had everything to do with real estate, land acquisition from married priests and nothing to do with anything spiritual. The church made the law and told no one how to deal with their sexuality; still hasn't, left everyone out there flapping in the fucking wind. What a travesty, what a legacy the church has left us: thousands and thousands of damaged children."

He starts to break up again but restrains.

"I was an alcoholic before I even became a priest. I was just modeling my dad, my mom, my friends, the neighborhood, church. In those days, seemed like alcoholism and Catholicism went hand in hand.

"So! Let's get down to it. I asked you to meet me here 'cause I got intrigued by Eliade's book on shamanism and those ecstatic episodes you were having. In an e-mail you sent a while ago you said that your lectures were now about tea as an ally plant, entheogen and therapeutic vehicle. Explain, and don't give me any shit about it." He laughs.

I was stunned. Michael had never opened like this before. Never. I thought I might need to stop and catch my breath, make tea, but he was on fire, on a roll, on a campaign. I decided to ride the wave, to keep going.

"Well, Michael, really, it's like everything else that one loves, respects, has a relationship with. It's about reciprocity. You pour your love into the tea leaves as they brew, or into an individual and there's a natural desire for that individual to respond to that love, to yield, whether it's another person or a plant or an animal. All an ally plant is, really, is a friend, a pal. I sometimes muse that tea, that all plants, are, in some way, plumbing the depths of our hearts and souls, nudging us toward growth, as if she, as this master plant, desires only the best for us, wanting to heal our broken hearts.

"Tea's an ally plant because of its beneficent effect on humanity. We've cultivated such an extraordinary friendship with this bush, this leaf, this plant, approached it with such reverence and respect, that there's no other plant about which we've created so many rituals and ceremonies. People that have used the term ally to help define tea's importance, however, have done it an injustice by using the term lightly and not taking it to the next level because that's a little more of a stretch. And that next level of what defines tea as an ally is something with which one connects or unites with in "A PERSONAL RELATIONSHIP." Now what that means is relative and may even be private. It was for me for years. I created my own private ritual for tea that was meaningful to me because like that lady, the anthropologist, Monica Wilson says, "Rituals reveal values at their deepest levels. People express in ritual what moves them most."

Michael's attention shifts. He pulls his energy back into himself. I pause and gave him some space.

68

A glint of sun catches something on Michael's sleeve. We both look down at the same time. A long black strand of hair lifts off his shirt and floats up into the air. It rolls and tumbles, shimmering, sparkling in the sun and disappears out over the river.

We were both dazzled by it, transfixed.

I had to assume that the hair was from a woman he'd been dating.

He took a deep breath. "Go on."

"First nation people, indigenous people, shamans, Taoists, Buddhists, go even further and describe plants as sentient beings. Now, it may be disputed that the substance contained within the lowly tea bag, no matter how dry and stale and pulverized, is a sentient being, but it is. And who determines that? You do.

"The term entheogen means "generating God within," or a substance that creates the sensation or an experience of the divine. It's a term that was created in the 1970's to describe a psychoactive or psychotropic substance used in religious, shamanic or spiritual contexts.

"Psychoactive/psychotropic substances are those which cause changes in "perception, mood, consciousness, cognition, and behavior." I've experienced altered and enhanced states in each of these categories with two types of China tea both from Yunnan Province: Pu-erh and the Dian Hongs or Yunnan Royal Gold. This is because they've been growing in situ, in their own native hills, in their own soils for millions of years, a lot longer than man ever walked the earth. No other tea growing anywhere on the planet can boast that!

"And therapeutic vehicle? When I take that first sip of tea, I often follow the warmth of the tea down into my tummy where the tea seems to pool and spread out. If you keep your energy and attention there, the caffeine will kick in, creating the sensation of waking up in your belly. It's a very different perspective from which to view the world, or yourself. In the altered, often magnified states that tea produces, you may, if you are inclined toward such things, find an opportune moment for some self-examination here.

"In my own private rituals, I pray over the leaves as they brew. I hold my palm over the leaves and run my energy, my chi into the tea. Sometimes, as I do this, "unsubdued elations," to coin a line from Wallace Stevens, may rise seeming to tailgate or piggyback the chi as it's moving around. Unresolved feelings may rise as well, bringing them to the fore for me to welcome home, so to speak.

"There are many portals that tea opens and invites us to enter. And this is where tea plays its most intimate role as our ally because, through all those doors, you are met time and again with tenderness and love, safety..........and wisdom. It really is all the joy and love that melts things, dissolves heartache, when your lips first break the surface tension of the brew and your whole body fills with the essence of the leaf. That essence is the love that we approach her with, this Thea Sinensis, this Goddess of China. We attend to her with our love, our devotion and she responds."

"In the tea establishment, there's a fondness for comparing tea with wine because it's convenient. Both are beverages we take into our mouths, discern with our palates and swallow.

"While it is said that there is truth in wine, there may only be a certain amount of truth until you get drunk. Then what kind of truth do you have?

"The truth is that wine and tea have nothing in common. Their methods of harvesting and processing are completely different: one's a leaf, the other a fruit. Their impact on our bodies is dissimilar: one's a stimulant, the other a depressant. It would be much more appropriate, although some might consider scandalous, controversial, to compare tea with another leaf which is also a stimulant, also an ally plant and entheogen used in religious, shamanic and spiritual contexts, a plant that has numerous healthful benefits and curative properties and who's harvesting and processing are nearly identical to tea: tobacco!

"Let's face it, these substances have been in use for trillions and trillions of years possibly even before Columbus discovered the earth."

Michael was still with me, making eye contact, nodding, smiling here and there.

"Are you alright? Would you like me to stop?"

"Nope. Go ahead."

"I'll tell you my tobacco story. Once, in a restaurant at the Stone Forest near Kunming, a group of us were sitting down to lunch when my attention was distracted by a sweet, unusual fragrance floating through the rooms. I turned around and saw a man smoking through a bong. I got up to take a closer look. It was a homemade contraption that had been soldered together from what looked like a number of tomato sauce cans. Still fascinated by the fragrance, I asked what it was he was smoking and was told it was tobacco. As I watched, I saw that he was unwrapping cigarettes and emptying them into the bowl of this makeshift pipe. The tobacco was a deep rich golden color unlike anything I'd ever seen and its fragrance unfamiliar to me. The bottom of the bong contained water through which the smoke was pulled. As the open top of the bong was quite wide, this man placed his whole mouth down into the top of the can as he held a match to the tobacco and breathed in. He noticed my interest, got up and offered me his chair that I might partake and partake I did. I breathed in a small quantity of the smoke to taste it and was amazed by its sweet, soft and soothing texture. It didn't look like tobacco, it didn't smell like tobacco and it certainly didn't taste like it. I was enchanted, curious, transfixed, puzzled by the extraordinary taste.

"Either later that day or the next we were at the Pu-erh tea factory in Menghai tasting and comparing Pu-erhs from the six tea mountains of the Xishuanbanna district. At an opportune moment, I asked an English-speaking member of the staff if he was familiar with this tobacco. He lit up, got excited, disappeared for half an hour, returned with a kilo of the stuff wrapped in newsprint and gave it to me. He'd also procured a whole box of rolling papers. My offer to pay was refused. I was stunned. How sweet!

71

"On further inquiry, I found that it was the local tobacco and Yunnan's largest cash crop. I could see why. It was delicious and I was a non-smoker.

"A traveling companion expressed an interest in my exploits and offered his hotel room as a place where we might partake.

"Unlike my room, his had a balcony and a view, a view of the 18,637 foot, snow-covered peak of Jade Dragon Snow Mountain. It was September and we were in Lijiang. And so we sat and rolled this matted shag-like gold into the papers I'd been given, Chinese rolling papers; smaller than those in the US and without any gum. So we just paused, gazed up at the mountain and were silent for quite some time.

"I kept the smoke in my mouth and swirled it all around, savoring the various taste sensations.

"It was a balmy evening, that night in Lijiang, as balmy as it is here now by the river.

"Sometimes I wonder if the plants and the rocks, the minerals themselves aren't somehow pointing the way back to our pre-Judeo-Christian roots. It reminds me of what Stephen Karcher did with the "I Ching." He purged it of Confucianism and returned it to its shamanic roots. I think the same thing should be applied to tea ceremonies. Purge them of humanity's conventions of them and have tea initiate us in ritual.

"When I first tried tobacco in ceremony, it was the local tobacco here in New Mexico called Punche, Punche de Mexicano, Nicotiana Rustica. It was a species that was brought north from Peru by the Spanish conquistadors hundreds of years ago. From what I understand, it's still cultivated on various Pueblo lands for ceremonial use. It's a potent leaf and is said to contain higher levels of nicotine than its North American brothers and sisters. It's also called Indian Tobacco. Anyway, when I first tried it, there was this subtle renting of the veil. The spirit world felt closer and I prayed to my relatives there, asked for their guidance.

"And then there's that double edged sword that these entheogenic substances present. The whole issue of abuse

72

and addiction where for some, tea and tobacco are medicines and for others they are poisons."

Michael's body tightens up and he gazes at me suspiciously.

"The addiction issue with tobacco's obvious but an addiction to tea's more subtle, insidious. Here, let me read you something I'm working on: "If all you're worried about in today's world is your addiction to caffeine then count your blessings. I'm not trying to minimize the problem, because caffeine is indeed addictive, but considering all the dangerous drugs out there, caffeine, packaged and delivered in the form of tea, is often talked about in the same breath as an addiction to chocolate. If caffeine is your drug of choice, than it may be more likely that you would be a coffee drinker, which has a lot more caffeine.

"There are all kinds of addictions in today's societies. There are people who love too much; there are people who work too much. The socially acceptable addictions of alcohol and tobacco are only acceptable to people whose lives have not been affected, or destroyed, by someone they love. An alcoholic friend of mine once said "We are all flawed, Frank." It was, I felt, a uniquely Christian thing for him to say and I didn't like being included in his view of the universe. We may all have issues, yes, but not all of us have pathologies. Unless, of course, Adam and Eve had pathologies, or maybe, more graciously, they were just fucked up."

Michael bursts out with his delightful laughter.

"As I've said before, if you already have an addictive personality it could present a problem but then so could most everything else. You can have a dysfunctional relationship with tea just like you can with people.

"That same alcoholic friend assured me that he had it all under control. Right. He thinks that he can outsmart his body by keeping one step ahead of beckoning emotional and spiritual issues by consuming more caffeine and racing ahead of his body's and his soul's needs, his soul's desires for himself. Doesn't work. Sooner or later it will all catch up with him.

"The bottom line was that he was self-medicating."

73

Michael eyes had glazed over. He was beginning to nod off because he didn't want to hear it.

I changed the subject to try to retrieve him.

"You mentioned Mircea Eliade? Here's one of his quotes: "What must be emphasized at once is that all these (plant) hierophanies point to a system of coherent statements, to a theory of the sacred significance of vegetation."

"Here's another from a student of alchemy and plant medicines, Frederick Dannaway, a tea colleague from Delaware: "Tea is not hallucinogenic, but it is certainly psychoactive with numerous medicinal and physiological properties producing energies and sensations far beyond what a reductionist study of the chemicals and alkaloids could reveal. We lack the vocabulary for substances that instantly give peace, inspire poetry or transport to a dreamy landscape with a single sip."

"Having been under the influences of rapid infusions of some 1950's Red Mark Yin-Ji Puerh I feel justified in suggesting tea or Camellia Sinensis as a possible candidate or substitute for Soma. With tiny orbs of qi coursing through my system after each sip I see a vision of the lineage of patriarchs of Esoteric Buddhas and thangkas of blue Bodhisattvas holding cups of amrita in their palm. Tea may not be the original soma, but the reverence, ritual and perhaps the shape into which it is pressed (especially in Tibet), make it a serious candidate as a soma-substitute or amrita."

Mr. Dannaway continues: "Drinking the "world in a bowl of tea," tracing the world in the hearth ashes, the tea-elixir's supreme mystery saturates, transmutes in the evolving process of internal communion. The central role of the "splendid tree from the South" in the hermit and literati traditions at the core of microcosmic aesthetics attests to the truly visionary energy sublimely lingering in every bowl and kettle. Sweet herb of the immortals, tea is truly the magic leaf that moves mountains into valleys."

And then he reminds us of this: "It is not only that there is water in the world, but there is a world in water. It is not just in water. There is a world of sentient beings in the clouds. There is a world of sentient beings in the air. There is a world of sentient beings in the fire... There is a world of sentient beings in a blade of grass." From the "Mountain and Water Sutra" by Dogen.

"And here's one from academia, from the King's College don, Alan MacFarlane. You never hear an intellectual talk like this:

"Tea became like the hallucinogenic drugs that have helped shamans in many other parts of the world to enter or communicate with the spirit world. It constituted the mystical center of the rites of withdrawal, self-abnegation and the attainment of nothingness in the new sects. To have its full effect, to release the maximum amount of caffeine and other relaxants and stimulants, tea had to be prepared in its purest and most powerful form. So it was ground into a powder and used as fresh as possible. It was also prepared and served in an almost sacred manner, emphasizing and encouraging the belief in its mystical power."

"From the book, *Tea of the Sages*, "These three uses for tea in early China—as an herb that promotes health, as a means to achieve heightened states of alertness, and as a beverage that, when ritually prepared, allowed communion with divinities, suggest the reasons for its continued appeal in later ages in both China and Japan."

"And lastly, one from the Reverend Michael O'Donnell, rector of St. Camellia's, after partaking of a new Wu Yi Bao Zhong, "This stuff rocks, Dude!""

Michael smiles. He was still with me but silent.

After a while comes this:

"You know what no one ever taught us to do? No one ever taught us to pour our love out into the Universe, pour our love out into the world to help the world with absolutely no expectation or attachment because we know that the Universe will do the rest. To do it even if we feel nothing, to have it on our lips and in our hearts at all times. We've always prayed TO GOD FOR THINGS, petitioning her for help. We sing praise, we give thanks but we don't viscerally transmit our love into the world. Pouring out love is not the old prayer-like petitioning-posture of "Oh, God, please help Johnny with his toothache" because we're not directing this transmission of love anywhere. We're using our body to access, generate and transmit that love into the world. It is the love of which we are all composed, the love which predates humanity, predates the earth and it is precisely this practice of pouring our love out into the world that becomes our social, political and spiritual activism. It's a prayer so powerful it alters my physiology, my brain chemistry to better practice it, accommodate it.

"With tea, there's a whole bunch of factors that figure into all these numinous, supernatural and transcendental experiences of tea you're always talking about. Central here is not your perfect practice, your precious porcelain, your impressive palate or the water that you use. Central to these variables is your willingness to be affected by the unknown, a willingness to be wakened from things you did not know you needed to be wakened from. A willingness to be wakened from things you DIDN'T WANT to be wakened from."

My mouth dropped open. I was so surprised, excited, at what was coming out of Michael that tears rolled down my cheeks. Here was the Michael I'd been waiting for.

"That's right, Frankie." He said, watching me with a smile. "I've not shared everything about myself with you until today, you old fart, because even though some people, such as yourself, consider tea to be a visionary substance, it doesn't have any of the dramatic "visuals" of other plant spirit medicines. It's too subtle and it's that subtlety that stills us, makes us want to stretch, lean forward and pay attention.

"Like you said, it truly is a stretch for some to consider that the substance contained within their tea bags is a sentient being but it is. We tend to project our dysfunction into everything we touch. The simple ritual of tea reminds me to simplify my life. Though our lives may be compli-cated, the ritual of tea is not, or at least, does not have to be.

"My rituals continue to evolve, too. They must, I feel, in order to stay alive, to stay vibrant and dynamic.

"It seems a lot of people have their own ideas of what a proper cup of tea is when in fact there's no such thing. It makes no difference whether you prefer a caramel English

Breakfast tea with Tasmanian Leatherwood honey, whipping cream and a splash of your favorite morning Scotch, or a day old Dragon Well. The soulful experience of tea will still come shining through.

"Things can sometimes get a little too serious in the tea world with all of its protocol and etiquette. That's what grates on me about the Japanese Tea Ceremony. Some rituals are a little too formal for me, a little too stiff. I don't like being self-conscious when I'm taking tea and I certainly don't like people watching my every move.

"If you couple all of these social conventions with a religion or a spiritual practice of some sort, things can get downright severe. The point is that, yes, once again, we forgot that when we first heard about tea it was in conjunction with another word that really set the mood for all future approaches and those two words, taken together, were:

"TEA PARTY"

"This is the mood I hope you create in your next book, Mister Murphy. Great belly laughs to break up all the solemnity, all the ways we take ourselves so damn seriously, all the stupid ass minutiae.

"People get so hung up with trying to discern what particular teas taste like that they miss the entire experience. They miss what tea, as a plant spirit medicine, has to teach us. There's no incentive to know. We've lost our way and now here we are, watching the planet dissolve before our eyes.

"We all know that the good Lord gifted humanity with this Divine Herb to reinforce our belief in the supernatural. Why is it then that we question the validity of our experience when we come face to face with the God of Abraham after 40 cups of tea?

The sun came up over the eastern rim of the canyon and everything turned gold.

VIII

CLOSED FOR RESOURCE PROTECTION

After breakfast, Michael confessed that he wanted to get back to Santa Fe. I was still dazed by all that he had shared. It felt like he had made peace with something on his retreat at the monastery. I wanted to hear more but it was not to be.

"I'll make us a pot of tea then," and just went ahead without any fuss.

"Let's let this brew till December," he joked with a wonderful smile.

"Gets cold long about then doesn't it?" I flashed.

There was a softness in his voice now that I'd never heard before, a kindness, and I could finally understand what made him so loved by all back there in Boston.

By this time we were both sitting looking out at the water in the two chairs I'd brought.

A bird shot past.

"What was that?" It startled Michael.

"That was a mountain bluebird!" I said. "Aren't they beautiful with that bright blue breast?"

"Look there!" I pointed to the ground a few feet from Michael.

A chip monk was sitting there chewing on some Cholla Cactus seeds with his back to us.

"Well, he's confident." Michael said.

He continued: "I was awake for a while last night and watched a shooting star come down and light up the entire face of that cliff over there with an eerie green glow," and he pointed across the river with his elbow.

"And I saw another break in two so that there were two shooting stars traveling alongside each other shooting off sparks like sparklers. Never seen that before."

"I'd like to smell one going by." I said excitedly.

"I'd like to have one land in my tea." Michael was almost giddy.

"I'd like to see a crop circle form on the surface of my tea."

We were back, bantering, playful. It was fun.

The tea was ready and I poured us both a cup of a Pu-erh I'd picked and made myself at the Menghai Factory years ago.

"Whoa!" Michael said on the first sip. "You're beginning to make it as intense as I do.'

"I'm still learning about what you like," I said with kindness and appreciation.

"No adulterants this morning, Michael?"

"Not this time."

"I like a tea so strong that it changes my moon and rising sign."

We giggle and almost start crying for God's sake.

"You know, I have to laugh at those Chinese tea men who say that tea diminishes their sexual desires. My experience is that it does just the opposite."

"Maybe that's what they tell their wives." I quip.

"Ouch." Michael says. "That's intense."

My nose starts to bleed from both nostrils.

"Too much Pu-erh." I say.

I plug both with a Kleenex I keep in the chest pocket of my shirt.

"The tea raised my yang AND my wang."

We chuckle again.

Gazing down into my teacup, I remarked that some Pu-erhs, such as this one, brew up blacker than coffee and how perfect that was to lure coffee drinkers over to tea, especially the ones that were casting about for alternatives.

Michael agrees.

"You know in all the tea books I've read there's never an unkind word about coffee. Not even a sarcastic aside. Tea people are too nice sometimes, too polite."

"It goes with the terrain." I share. "May I have your permission to change that unspoken agreement right now, Mr. Mick?"

79

"Be my guest."

"Alright," I say, all animated, about to launch into a homily all my own.

"Truth is, coffee's a gateway drug and leads to heroin addiction. It's the drink of felons."

Michael turns and looks at me with anticipation.

"How's that?" he plays along.

"All those heroin addicts I interviewed for that research I was doing about opium?"

"Go on."

"Every single one of them started with coffee!"

"No shit?"

"No shit."

"Well, then, there we have it!"

"Amen."

All of a sudden, we start hearing these tinny, whirling sounds rushing past and crashing into the trees. Some landed in the river. They were mechanical birds "flying," gliding overhead.

"It's Fanny Leibowitz!" I tell Michael. "She's trying to get my attention with her wind up inventions."

I stand up with my binoculars, scan the mesa behind us, catch her on a promontory and wave. She waves back indicating she'll be down in an hour or two.

"You've not met Fanny yet have you? She'll be down in a while."

"Gotta go." Michael was getting anxious.

Michael got up grabbing his picnic basket and his French beach chair, the driver's seat of his Citroen. We walked up to his car together and for the very first time I realized I was going to miss him.

"Do those contraptions of hers ever hit you?"

"Never. They're laser guided, or something, like smart bombs."

"Oh, that's reassuring, she from LANL (Los Alamos National Laboratory)?"

"Yep."

"I don't want to meet anyone named Fanny. And you know what else? How about all those scientists up there on the hill look for the "Love Particle" instead of the "God Particle," that Higgs-Boson thing? How about they isolate that particle, speed it up in an accelerator and bombard humanity's tumors with love instead of all this crippling radiation?"

"Brilliant, Michael!"

He smiled and, for a moment, I thought he was going to kiss me on the forehead.

With a quick hug, he opened the door, snapped the seat in place and got in. He turned on the engine and shifted into reverse by pulling a rod straight out from the dashboard and turning it. We smiled and shook hands through the car window. He then backed the Deux Chevaux out onto the road and headed back to Santa Fe.

A couple of days later, his heart gave out and he was gone.

I marked my place in his journals with a blade of grass and put them down on the ground.

I thought of some lines from Li Po:

THE BIRDS HAVE VANISHED INTO THE SKY
AND NOW THE LAST CLOUD DRAINS AWAY.
WE SIT TOGETHER, THE MOUNTAIN AND I
UNTIL ONLY THE MOUNTAIN REMAINS.

And then, another poem came to mind.

YOU WERE FOREORDAINED TO FIND THE SOURCE.
NOW, TRACING YOUR WAY AS IN A DREAM
THERE WHERE THE SEA FLOATS UP TO THE SKY,
YOU WANE FROM THE WORLD IN YOUR FRAGILE
BOAT.....
THE WATER AND THE WIND ARE AS CALM AS YOUR
FAITH,
FISHES AND DRAGONS FOLLOW YOUR CHANTING,
AND THE EYE STILL WATCHES BEYOND THE HORIZON
THE HOLY LIGHT OF YOUR SINGLE LANTERN.

("Farewell to a Japanese Buddhist Priest Bound Homeward" by Tang Dynasty poet, Ch'ien Ch'i. (Qian Qi, 710–782)) from "The Jade Mountain" translated by the late Santa Fe poet, Witter Bynner.

They said Michael died of congestive heart failure but it might as well have been congestive heartache for all the doctor's knew.

I sat in my chair gazing out at the river for several days. I felt like I could sit there all winter.

There were a number of signs posted up and down the road by the National Forest Service. Old campsites and parking areas were now declared off limits because of human infraction. The signs all said the same thing: CLOSED FOR RESOURCE PROTECTION. It was how I felt at times, after a certain amount of overuse by the general public. "Sorry everyone. I'm closed to protect my resources. See you in the spring."

IX

"THE NOTES"

So after a few days I reached back down, picked up Michael's journals and started in again. Since there were all these miscellaneous notes, I organized them under what I hoped would be relevant headings.

These would be the notes referred to in the title of this book.

HUMOR

To enhance one's tea drinking pleasure, it is essential to have sex before, during and after tea.

And then, all of a sudden-like, I realized it would be exceedingly beneficial if I were to have some Cheese Puffs before I threw the "I Ching."

The monkeys that pick our tea shower first.

"Reality is for people who can't tolerate drugs." Lily Tomlin

So how did you like that green tea?
I liked the hot water part.

Drink tea and nourish life.
With the first sip, joy.
With the second, satisfaction.
With the third, Danish." Zen Judaism

"In certain trying circumstances, urgent
circumstances, desperate circumstances, profanity furnishes
a relief denied even to prayer." Mark Twain

Once I watched a woman, a very impatient woman,
pick up a hot teapot and swirl it around. She thought that by
so doing, she would be able to hurry the steeping process
along. That way, she wouldn't be so horribly inconven-
ienced. Silly American.

I understand that there's a town in New Mexico
named after the Tao?
There's a town in New Mexico named after a number
of Taos.

I can pray better now that I got my new espadrilles.

"Be Beer Now!"

Even though Peking Man was aware of his inability to
procure for himself a sterling silver tea service, he somehow
managed to persevere and overcome his karmic destiny as a
human being by stripping the branches of the trees and
placing live tea leaves directly into his mouth, forever
shaming modern man with all of his clever manipulations of
the leaf.

Two friends begin their tea books by mentioning opium but neither ever invite you over for any. With the American government heavily invested in Afghanistan's opium production, you'd think there'd be more available than what the CIA sells privately.

Yin Zhen and Yang Zen.

Insane and Outsane.

In order to make yourself appear to be a serious tea drinker, soak your dentures in Pu-erh every night.

"Is there any time of year when the local meteorologists are more accurate in predicting the weather here?"
"When they remember to take their meds."

"My girlfriend followed her morning tea with a coffee chaser."
"And how long did that relationship last, Michael?"
'Well, I was hopeful that the moment I saw her splash a little Southern Comfort in her tea that she'd be a keeper, but it didn't turn out to be the case."

"Irritable" is a gracious word, is it not, when your body seizes up in a toxic caffeine fit?

Epiphanies come during periods of great stress. Correction: Epiphanies come during periods of psychotic fucking breakdowns.

The taste of lead inside my hand-painted gaiwan aids my mercuric deciphering.

I hope you will find in these notes the pure joy and celebration of tea. And if you find that the tea I have made for you is not to your liking, well hey, there's a cuspidor right there at your feet and you may expectorate at your discretion without judgment or blame. You may do the same with my humor if you feel so inclined.

MICHAEL'S PERSONAL NOTES

Even destitution can be a form of monasticism.

All puffed up in their inflammatory conjunctions.

The incomprehensible demoralization of addiction.

So lost in reverie that I didn't want to have to go all the way up to my mind to try to figure out what kind of animal it was that just ran through the campsite.

My body is my guru.

Find that place in your body where love resides and rest there.

It's self-incineration offered up as a form of community service when spiritual leaders are challenged, publicly, on stage.

I was always concerned about rinsing tea and, at one time, thought it was done to subdue her, the divine feminine, to lessen her mystical impact.........that it was yet another way to minimize, to manipulate the divine feminine to serve the patriarchy.

Otium Sanctum, Holy Leisure

A monastic by temperament, I was reclusive by choice but when I used the word "reclusive" I found I had to temper it, qualify it a bit because people wondered, late at night, privately to themselves, if there was not a pathology attached. I keep them guessing. Proclivities toward eccentricism have their liberties but at a price. Adhering to the social mores of tea etiquette has been a challenge so I don't adhere at all.

IRREVERANT STATEMENTS

From a Korean tea book comes the phrase "A scholar is generally regarded as a man of virtue." Unless, of course, he's an asshole, in which case, he's not regarded at all.

Tealeaf reading: Eviscerate the contents of your tea bags, pour them onto the floor and read that!

Are aged oolong teas really aged..........or just stale?

Fresh water and English tea considered as oxymoronic.

Statement from an unnamed tea company: Japan's Fukushima nuclear disaster happened on 11 March 2011. The Japanese government and its corporations mislead the global community as to how serious and how extensive the radioactive contamination was and continue to do so today. We will, therefore, not carry any Japanese tea for a period of 30-40 years.

Sign on the road: Non-Catholic Burritos Ahead.

Every church needs a bar attached to it.

"No, ma'am, I'm not here on retreat. I'm here to observe the mating rituals of monastic clergy."

If it weren't for caffeine and aspirin my entire theology would collapse.

With all "the stuff," all the fancy tea ware and all the codified affectations, the Japanese Tea Ceremony ends up supplanting and upstaging the tea.

"Most books about tea make nice kindling." Michael O'Donnell

QUOTES

"There were times when I could not afford to sacrifice the bloom of the present moment to any work, whether of the head or hands. I love a broad margin to my life. Sometimes, in a summer morning, having taken my accustomed bath, I sat in my sunny doorway from sunrise till noon, rapt in a reverie, amidst the pines and hickories and sumacs, in undisturbed solitude and stillness, while the birds sang around or flitted noiseless through the house, until by the sun falling in at my west window, or the noise of some traveler's wagon on the distant highway, I was reminded of the lapse of time. I grew in those seasons like corn in the night, and they were far better than any work of the hands would have been. They were not time subtracted from my life, but so much over and above my usual allowance. I realized what the Orientals mean by contemplation and the forsaking of works. For the most part, I minded not how the hours went. The day advanced as if to light some work of mine; it was morning, and lo, now it is evening, and nothing memorable is accomplished. Instead of singing like the birds, I silently smiled at my incessant good fortune. As the sparrow had its trill, sitting on the hickory before my door, so had I my chuckle or suppressed warble which he might hear out of my nest."

Thoreau

"Don't surround yourself with yourself!" Anderson Bruford Wakeman Howe

"Truth, the ultimate Tao, is not earned. It bursts from your heart."   Ivan M. Granger

"Tea is a ritual-causing agent. Continuous engagement in the ceremonial experience initiates you, apprentices you." Carol Parker

"Stability in cheerfulness is stronger than fate."
I Ching

"That which brings light must endure burning."
Rumi

"If you can't pray a real prayer, pray hypocritically, full of doubt and dry mouthed. God accepts counterfeit money, as though it were real!" Rumi

"Consider what you are about to say, and ask yourself if it is an improvement on silence." Swami Kripalvanandji

"Your task is not to seek for love, but merely to seek and find all the barriers within yourself that you have built against it." A Course in Miracles. A nod to Hugh Prather's "Dispensable Church," Santa Fe, NM.

"Our real journey in life is interior: it is a matter of growth, deepening and an ever greater surrender to the creative action of love and grace in our heart."
Thomas Merton

"That is, at bottom, the only courage that is demanded of us: to have the courage for the most strange, the most singular and the most inexplicable that we may encounter. That mankind has, in this sense, been cowardly has done life endless harm; the experiences that are called "visions" the whole so-called "spirit world," death, all those things that are so closely akin to us have, by daily parrying, been so crowded out of life that the senses with which we could have grasped them are atrophied. To say nothing of God."

Rainer Maria Rilke

"Nowhere can man find a quieter or more untroubled retreat than in his own soul." Marcus Aurelius

"A little while alone in your room will prove more valuable than anything else that could ever be given you."   Rumi

"Forget safety. Live where you fear to live. Destroy your reputation. Be notorious. I have tried prudent planning long enough. From now on I'll be mad."   Rumi

ORGANIZED RELIGIONS, SCIENCE AND THE WESTERN MIND

Scientists have concluded that Catholicism doesn't work.

Mystics have concluded that science doesn't work.

We've mind everything out of existence.

"Nothing can be found by intellectual processes."
P.D. Ouspensky

Western man has become "the whore of reason" and sacrificed his soul for his mind. In so doing, he has destroyed the earth and needs to cultivate a "dialogue with non-European spiritual traditions (which would) lead us to rediscover certain neglected sources of our own spiritual heritage," (paraphrased from Mircea Eliade). A return to shamanism empowers everyone.

Tea, too, needs to be purged of its human conventions and returned to its shamanic roots.

I stepped up to the lectern, announced that I was going to be jumping around a bit and addressed myself to the faeries of the glade. As my mental holdings waned, I was beginning to believe in those little woodland spirits more and more. They make a hell of a lot more sense to me than anything science could come up with.

Think regressive hypnotherapy is hip? Try regressing back to the plant life of Yunnan Province.

NATURE OBSERVATION

Fire prevention sign once posted at the entrance to Forest Service Road 151: "Think you can't go camping without a campfire? Try camping without a forest."

LETTER TO THE EDITOR THAT WAS PUBLISHED IN THE NEW MEXICAN NEWSPAPER: If NM's river rafting companies continue to desecrate the vegetation in the Chama River Wild and Scenic Area by creating their own roads wherever it pleases them to do so, then more and more areas will be closed to the public, as some already are, and the access roads to our favorite spots will be blocked with signs that say "Closed for Resource Protection." Wise up!

Cryptogamic soil, also called cryptobiotic soil, is "an extraordinary community of mutual consent." It's that dark brown or black raised crust on the ground. Cryptogamic means a "hidden marriage" between lichen, fungi, algae and moss. Try not to step on it.

I watched a tiny spider silking down from a tree but the amount of silk she was releasing to get to the ground seemed many more times greater than her body weight. How is that possible?

With the sun low in the west, thousands of pebbles, a quarter of an inch in diameter, were casting long, needle-like shadows on the surface of the road.

There are lots of swifts and swallows here that tear ass around at dusk catching insects, particularly mosquitoes. One snapped past my left ear once as I sat motionless on the bluff. Scared the shit out of me. Felt like he was doing about 40 MPH.

Just as tea is an ally plant for humanity, we, as a species, need to be allies to the earth.

Nothing like a fall off a craggy cliff to realign my vertebrae.

TEA OBSERVATIONS

When some tea leaves are exposed to metal or touch metal, their chi retracts back into the midrib of the leaf and it becomes more effortful to coax their flavors out, a flavor that may, on the first infusion, taste weak. Subsequent infusions may also taste strained depending on how forceful or impatient one is.

When I brew The Dian Hong in glass, and all the leaves gather as in a bog on the surface, I gaze up underneath the leaves to watch descending clouds of amber dropping to the bottom of my vessel. You can't behold that in a pot or lidded gaiwan.

If you want to feel tea mobilizing the chi, or qi, in your body, try this: Make yourself a strong cup, lay down in bed to rest and pay attention. Pay attention with your body not your mind.

White caps on my tea.

When the timer went off, I dipped a wooden spoon into my tea and it pulled the entire surface tension down with it as if it were a thin membrane, a layer of silk, that had spread itself out upon the surface of my tea.

In the desert, clouds of steam form just beneath the surface tension of my tea looking for a way out.

A hummingbird whirls up from the river and stares into the red floral patterns of my gaiwan with profound expectation.

The cancelling ripples on the surface of my tea, jostling about in my car's cup holder, ripple out and ripple in as I drive down the road.

I whipped up a cup of Kitchen Matcha and sat it on the dash, steaming up the front windshield as I pulled back up onto one fifty one.

You don't need to decorate your tea.

If you're tired, take a nap. If you're thirsty, drink water. Satisfy your body's basic needs first. Then rejoice in tea.

Chase your tea with a full glass of water. You'll lose some of the lingering aftertaste but it'll help ease the strain on your kidneys, liver and adrenals caused by the caffeine.

On page 115 of Kit Chow's "All the Tea in China," we find this: "Never use tea that has stood over night. Researchers at the Fujian Province Chinese Medicine Research Institute found that while fresh green and oolong tea lowered incidence of lung cancer in rabbits, green tea that stood overnight increased it."
Let's see some intrepid soul talk about that at the World Tea Expo!

If you're so anxious to bestow the title of tea master upon someone, you can start with the farmers!

There never were any indigenous tea trees in India, therefore, the term Assamica should be discarded.

Sometimes your tea is only as good as your water.

I'm cautious about saying anything derogatory about any tea because, if a tea is of poor quality, it is of poor quality most often because of the decisions made by the people that produced it.

Tea's enduring, universal appeal to our calmer, more quiet natures solicits the best in all of us.

The afterglow of tea, that all pervading sense of wellbeing.

You would be hard pressed to find a homeopath who has ever prescribed the homeopathic remedy made from tea, *Thea Sinensis*. This is because the symptoms for which it is recommended do not often constellate together. In fact, the symptoms are polar opposites, ranging from murderous impulses to feelings of euphoria and exaltation. Can you imagine someone with this latter symptom going to a doctor and saying, "Gee, Doc, I'm feeling a little exalted lately. Do you have anything to bring me down?"

It is the former end of the spectrum, similar to extreme caffeine toxicity, that is more troubling: the fear you are going to murder your children or your whole family. Tea itself has the capacity to relax AND stimulate, beyond our comfort level. It is a conundrum, is it not, that two of the largest tea producing countries in the world, China and India, have the highest rates of infanticide? Dare we ask if there's a connection?

The ultimate tea experience really depends on whether you want to fill your head with data or fill your heart with wisdom.

About tea, there are no rules, no edicts, no canon laws. You won't be prosecuted for making a faux pas. You won't be condemned because all you're doing is taking a bunch of leaves and placing them in some hot water. What's so intimidating about that?

The Spanish expression "No me entra bien" or "It doesn't enter well," said of wine, may also be said of tea. It may also be interpreted as "It doesn't come in well."

MY OWN NOTES

I prefer the taste of sleep to the taste of tea.

When I begin to feel the caffeine and its significant other, adrenaline, pool around my thyroid and begin to tax it and, at the same time, feel my heart begin to palpitate, I move the energy, or chi, of these two stimulants elsewhere to relieve the stress. All it takes is a few moments of going inside to create alternate spaces within which they may harbor.

The muffin had a bulbous top and slender slinking waist like a gaiwan. It was easy to confuse the two if you mislaid your spectacles or had a bit too much to drink.
"Is that a gaiwan over there, Frank?"
"No, it's a muffin. Are you alright?"

Not too long ago, Michael told me of an experience he had with a Pu-erh. He said he saw a flash of light soon after he'd had a cup and that this beam felt like it had pierced something deep inside him, something he'd forgotten about, that it had unlocked something. He said the experience permitted him to breathe in a way he hadn't been able to since he was three and he drew a great long breath as he spoke these words. Perhaps something similar to this happened on his retreat. At this point, I could only guess.

There is a way that may be discerned between the dark, assertive forces of the universe and those that are more soft and yielding. There are teas that solicit these forces from us and magnify them, and there are teas that subdue those forces. The way of tea is the middle way, discovering the balance within it all.

Tea is a sentient being. Why not approach her as such? The wisdom that issues from her may not come from her leaves alone but from her guild. Indeed, it may come from the entire plant "kin-dom."

We hang on the words of our ancient "masters" not realizing that our own intuitive wisdom may be more accurate.

You can spend your whole life filling your mind with technical data about tea but would it not behoove thee, would it not be more beneficial to humanity, to let this master plant enter your soul and waken the intelligence of your heart?

Sometimes I feel that man's manipulation of tea has corrupted its essence, that the more manipulated the leaf, the more challenging it is to discern tea's soul because of all the distractions that detain us on the way to that essence. We might say that the more altered, the more doctored a tea, the more flavorful it is, the more caffeine it contains, the more potent it's effects upon us. All of these things aren't bad but they can inhibit our search for tea's divinity. The truth is that tea's soul shines forth no matter what we do to it, no matter how profound man's clever presence has embedded itself into the leaf.

There's a lesson here, for the same is true for us. We are molded, shaped, "manipulated" by life, by the choices we make. We are bruised, roughed up, rolled and withered but our central cores remain the same. We, like tea, just pull ourselves back into the stem to survive and it is there, that we eventually discover our strength, our truth, our kinship with all life.

He doesn't have a palate.
No, he just doesn't have your palate.

When I got home I made myself a cup of tea, or at least tried to. It isn't so bad having to blow cat hairs out of the bottom of my gaiwan before I use it but having to pluck them out with a spatula after I've already made the tea blackens my mood. And then, just as I'm about to take my first sip, I hear the unmistakable crunch of a bird's skull as my hunter/gatherer cat hauls in the morning kill. And just as I've removed both cat and carnage and settled back down to tea, my two year old son clears the kitchen table of my entire tea service with his shoe.

I would ask sometimes if it were possible to learn about love, to learn about patience and compassion from a plant and the answer always returns with a resounding "YES!"

Tea needs to be infused by us, not just by water.

To say that we are anything less than love is a lie and leads to pathologies. To say that we cannot all have direct and immediate experiences of the divine is a lie and leads to pathologies.

When they make their final transitions, suicides, even murderers, will be met with love.

I'd like to see the application of Shou or Ripe Pu-erh manufacturing techniques used on non-Pu-erh varietals in India, Kenya and Argentina. Is that so far-fetched? What would that taste like?

If you are adept at tracking energy in your body then you may also be adept at tracking emotions as well. Try then tracking tea's effects as it opens all the little doors in your soul, for we may track tea's subtle influences not only on the palate but throughout our whole body.

Have your mouth, indeed, your entire sensorium reach for tea.

Ritual space pivots in a posture of reciprocity. When I came home, here to the oaks, I would always marvel at how the trees bowed with unceasing reverence to the river, bowed in gratefulness to the river for their life, their sustenance. Their presence, their deportment, was always greater than that of any human occupation in the glade. I would go up to them and hug them so they could feel my affection for them, my devotion. They made the entire grove a ritual space.

The distant thud of a large bore rifle broke my concentration and I remembered it was hunting season on the mesas above. It was getting late. I was cold, tired, and my thoughts had begun to turn towards home.

I'd stay one more night and head back to Santa Fe before dawn.

X

"STOP DRINKING ME." The Tea Plant

"All of man's troubles stem from his inability to sit
quietly in a room by himself." Blaise Pascal

I woke at four and lay staring up into the night. Stars
sparkled through the trees and the smells of the earth reminded me of another line from fellow New Englander,
Henry David Thoreau: "Morning air! If men will not drink of
this at the fountainhead of the day, why then, we must even
bottle up some and sell it in the shops for the benefit of those
who have lost their subscription ticket to morning time in
this world."

I took a number of great long breaths, filled myself
with this morning air and began to assess the day ahead.
Should I pack up and leave now or wait till daylight?

This time of year, driving the back roads of northern
New Mexico in the dark like this, I would have to watch for a
number of things. There may be pieces of firewood that had
fallen onto the road from overloaded pickup trucks. The
driver of the car ahead may decide to stop, jump out and
grab those pieces. These days, the only people doing this
were single moms on their way to work.

Livestock in the road was another issue, or deer and
coyotes bolting across it.

The most challenging aspect of night driving, even at
this hour, was our drunk drivers. If I'm not mistaken, I think
they appear on the state seal of New Mexico. So when I saw
a car coming, I, like everyone else, pulled way over to the
right to let them pass.

And, as a result of our drunk drivers, there were these
roadside memorials, or descansos, marking where people
had died in car accidents. Some were illuminated with low
voltage lighting, making them appear to be an array of

candles burning along the road. Some of the more elaborate ones, say where a number of people had perished, were quite distracting if you didn't know where they were.

On the brighter side, there were pleasant memories to recall as well when driving US Highway 84 in these pre-dawn hours.

Once, near Medanales, I came around a corner and there was a car stopped in the middle of the road. I pulled up behind and saw an elderly woman assisting a huge beaver cross the road so it could get back into the river.

Another time, dropping down into the village of Arroyo Seco, south of Espanola, I started smelling freshly brewed coffee. It puzzled me because I knew there weren't any cafes open here at this hour. As I descended into the valley, I realized that what I thought was coffee was, in fact, a skunk, puzzling me even more. I wondered if there were perhaps some sort of underlying, base fragrance they shared. There were indeed, I found out later, compounds, mercaptans, that they had in common.

All these things passed through my mind and I decided to wait till daylight.

As first light approached, the shifting fragrances of the canyon, accentuated by the morning's moisture, stimulated all my senses. I thought of the line "Pu-erhs.........which smelled like humus soaked by a summer rain." by Katrina Avila Munichiello, and my thoughts began to turn toward tea.

Here, too, there were a number of things to consider. Where was I in my body, for instance? Was I not comfortable, was I not satisfied enough at the moment, to just lay there quietly without getting up for another hour or two? Did I want to move from one space into another and what might that space be? Did I want to alter my mood, my temperament? If I had tea at this hour of the day, what would my chi, my energy and vitality be like later? It wasn't always a mental process, these deliberations, but one of just going inside and checking in. I was already in an altered space of heightened awareness being in this wilderness setting. How much more "amplified" did I want to be?

103

I thought of friends, more purist than I, who heated their water over charcoal fires in stone kettles. Reductionist in temperament, they felt all they required from life was water, a heating element, a few leaves and a vessel in which to brew them.

For my part, when I made tea in the woods, I sometimes left the lid off my brewing vessels. It made the tea cool differently, taste better. Perhaps it had something to do with how the steam evaporated as it rolled off the surface of the tea, or maybe it was how the brewing leaves aerated, mingling as they were, with the thin desert air. It may even have been that the tea was absorbing some of the chi from these surroundings. I certainly was.

I threw back my bed covers, got up and went over to my chair.

Long pink clouds radiated out from the eastern horizon and I thought of the line "The rosy fingered dawn," from Homer's *Iliad*.

The beauty of the canyon was having its own effect on me as I opened to it. It had pierced my heart, disarming me, short-circuiting my mind, making me more fragile, more vulnerable than I already was.

As I yielded to it and went out to meet it, a door opened and a voice came through that said, "Stop drinking me."

....

There's this dragging effect that the river has of pulling the earth down with it as it passes through the canyon. I stare at the water and there's a sensation of having things extracted from me, that the river is pulling things out of me. I gaze into the river and my mind flows out into it. It had the same quality that hot water has on tea leaves as they brew, eliciting from her all of her virtuous qualities. Perhaps this was what tea was asking of me. I feel all this now as I sit

104

here, alone, on this promontory above the river. Notions, trappings flying off, replaced with a revitalizing sense of strength that rushes in to fill the void. It is a rendering, this. My heart, too, lightened of its grief.

When Michael died a year ago, I stopped praying for him and started praying to him because he had become another kind of ally on the other side of the veil. I knew what gifts grief beheld, for when the heart is broken it is also open to receive the gifts of the divine.

I'd had mystical experiences all my life but never knew why, and now, as I aged, they were becoming more numerous, more intense. In light hearted moments I thought perhaps they were the result of having idled away my youth on the beaches of Martha's Vineyard, which naturally predisposed me to a silent, sensate life of no mind. No, not like Zen. I laid on the beach till I started sweating, played in the water till my lips turned purple, came up on dry land, plopped down and pulled that hot sand up all around me and sacrificed my life to the sun. Summers were easy on the Vineyard at twelve.

Oh, I could reach down into the back pocket of my swim trunks for my mind, swish it around in sea water to rouse it some and flourish in intellectual circles, but there was always this distrust of the mind, the feeling that I couldn't do spirituality with it.

I thought, too, that perhaps my innate sense of love was imparted to me from the earth itself as I laid upon it all those years in my youth. Remember the earth? It was what we all worshipped, what we all gleaned our wisdom from before we got so smart.

And then in comes this message to stop drinking tea.

I had only just begun to address myself to this plant as the spirit guide she'd been all along, soliciting her for her guidance as I moved through changes in my life. I was praying to her as the sentient being that she is. This was a much different approach than praying over the leaves, pouring my love and gratitude, my chi, into them as they brewed, something I'd done for 20 years.

My spirituality and mysticism weren't intellectual processes. Neither were they scholarly or academic pursuits. They are not of the mind because there's no logic in the numinous world. Deductive reasoning doesn't work here. My experiences of the divine haven't come gift wrapped in socially acceptable language. They just come.

I like my mind, don't get me wrong, I just attribute my experiences to the willful disuse of it.

On the material plane, one morning, with a little more acuity than usual, I noticed all the herbal remedies and elixirs I'd bought to help me, my body, process tea or, more accurately, tea's caffeine. (I do make a rather strong cup for myself.) There was Thyroidenum 30X, Camomilla 30c, Adrenotonic, Eleuthro (Siberian Ginseng), L-Theanine (Suntheanine), Kava, and a few more.

There were pharmacological issues. Years of caffeine ingestion had compromised my adrenals, my thyroid, indeed, my entire endocrine system.

Tea's caffeine had also made me tense and irritable, not a good posture within which to elicit a relationship with spirit, or other human beings for that matter.

Then there were the explosive pieces of investigative journalism Greenpeace did in 2012 on the excessive use of pesticides and, in some cases illicit pesticides, on tea in China. (There's been a lot of denial about this, the use of pesticides on tea in the entire global tea community.) It shed new light on why some tea enthusiasts may rinse their tea. With this in mind, the idea of rinsing tea leaves before you brew them may be but an illusion as pesticides would more apt to be inside the leaf, not upon them. Rains, mists, would wash pesticides off the leaves and onto the ground where they would be drawn up into the tea plants through their root systems. This is partly why I only do "THE FIRST INFUSION." Anything more than that almost feels toxic.

There was this devastating emptiness and loneliness when I stopped drinking. I had filled myself up with tea and left room for little else. The surprise held in the mystery of this command was the gift of the emptiness itself. For not only was I asked to stop drinking, I was asked to bask, to bathe in the emptiness that was now upon me.

Some, unnerved by this emptiness and the shattering anxieties that ensued, fell into the unconscious fears that drove them in the first place and began to fill these spaces with drugs or alcohol, food or sex, electronic media, the usual crutches, the usual suspects. This was the face of addiction but, after a while, they began to realize they had betrayed themselves by postponing their lives and, eventually, their personal work began again.

"Don't fill up all the empty spaces in your soul where spirit may enter. Don't fill these holes with your own personal host of habits and distractions or you may miss an opportunity that may not come again." She also said.

For years I had been riding high on the euphoria tea imparted. I wasn't conscious that I had been filling in all these empty spaces, didn't even know there was more emptiness to explore. The realization was that, in the end, the emptiness nourished me on levels that tea could not and I was now the vessel within which all of this would unfold.

For years I prayed, "...and I shall endeavor to create within myself a receptive vessel in which to receive that wisdom...." and now, here it was on my doorstep.

Perhaps there was a different type of wisdom the plant kingdom was wishing upon me, asking me to explore. I may have had my own intentions for myself but "Spirit" had a different agenda. Tea, the tea plant, perhaps an aspect of myself, had asked me to stop, to enable something else to come through.

So, in an instant, my agreements, my relationship with tea, with myself, had changed and I understood Sen No Rikyu's pronouncement, "Though many people drink tea, if you do not know the Way of Tea, tea will drink you up."

I wasn't asked to cut back, to be more moderate. I had been asked to it give up altogether.

And when I tried to "sneak out behind the barn" another voice came through and said "Enough" and that was that. It was done.

Now I get to sit quietly in a room by myself and wait.

APPENDIX

The first English translation of Li Po's only poem about tea.

Considering how often he was drunk, I always wondered why Li Po (Li Bo, Li Bai, 701-762 AD) never penned an ode to tea. It would've been, I imagine, the first thing he made for himself in the morning after an evening's indulgence, drinking as he so often did, alone, in the woods with the moon his only companion. And then, in a book called *Tao of Chinese Tea* by Huang Lingyun, I saw a reference to a poem about tea that Li Po wrote called variously, "Jade Spring Cactus Tea," or just "Cactus Tea." A friend in Taiwan sent it to me upon my inquiry. She was familiar with it but, as far as anyone knew, it had never been translated into English. I solicited Steven Owyoung, who worked from the original Chinese literary script of the Tang Dynasty. Steven's piece turned into an essay, the entirety of which may be viewed at Corax's chadao.blogspot.com dated April 19th, 2011.

From Mr. Owyoung's essay: "Immortal's Palm Tea was noted as the first poem to incorporate the actual name of a tea in its verse. The poem was also one of the earliest accounts of dry, loose leaf tea and Li Bo was the first poet to describe the sundried finishing of the leaf and its peculiar shape and form. Tang tea masters like Lu Yü generally used a highly refined, solid, dried paste of tea in the form of a small cake or wafer. Washed, steamed, pressed, pulped, and baked, caked tea was highly processed. Unlike cakes or wafers, the whole leaf of Immortal's Palm tea was slowly dried by the sun and retained nearly all of its natural oils, nutrients, and potency."

Immortal's Palm Tea

Ever have I heard of Mount Jade Spring,
Of its mountain grottos filled with stalactite caves
And immortal bats as big as white crows,
All hanging down above the clear, moonlit stream.
Tea grows among the rocks
And along Jade Spring's ceaseless flow.
Root and stem exude a rich fragrance;
One whiff nurtures flesh and bone.
Lush and voluminous, the green leaves;
Branch upon branch, row upon row.
The sun dries Immortal's Palm,
Coddling it like Hong Ya's shoulder.
The world has never seen the like,
But who will spread its name?
Nephew Ying, the Zen master
Presents this tea and a beautiful poem;
Both are bright mirrors embellishing ugly Wuyen,
But I am shamed by the beauty Xizi.
Even so, this morning I joyfully
Sing this song to the Heavens.

Made in the USA
San Bernardino, CA
30 June 2015